First published in Great Britain in 1992 by
Anaya Publishers Ltd,
Strode House, 44–50 Osnaburgh Street, London NW1 3ND

This edition published 1996 by Brockhampton Press,
a member of Hodder Headline PLC Group

Copyright © Collins & Brown 1996

Managing Editor: Janet Illsley
Photographer: James Murphy
Designer: Pedro Prá-Lopez
Food Stylist: Mary Cadogan
Background Artist: Annabel Playfair

British Library Cataloguing in Publication Data
Cadogan, Mary
Easy to cook pasta. – (Easy to cook)
641.8

ISBN 1 86019 225 4

Typeset in UK by SX Composing Ltd, Rayleigh
Colour reproduction by J. Film Process, Bangkok
Printed in UK by BPC Paulton Books Ltd

NOTES

Ingredients are listed in metric and imperial measures.
Use either set of quantities but not a mixture of both.

All spoon measures are level:
1 tablespoon = one 15 ml spoon
1 teaspoon = one 5 ml spoon.

Dried pasta is used unless otherwise specified.

Use fresh herbs and freshly ground black pepper unless otherwise stated.

Use standard size 3 eggs unless otherwise suggested.

CONTENTS

INTRODUCTION

Pasta is so perfect for the busy cook that it is hard to imagine life without it. Not only is it quick to cook, cheap, easy to store and good for you, it can be made into so many delicious and diverse dishes that it is almost impossible to tire of it!

The origins of pasta date back to the Greeks and Etruscans, and there is evidence that the Romans were eating laganum, a type of lasagne, as far back as 5 BC. Originally a speciality enjoyed only by the wealthy, it wasn't until the eighteenth century that pasta became an everyday food. In the early part of this century Italians emigrated to America in their millions and the popularity of pasta spread.

The best dried pasta is made from durum wheat, an exceptionally hard wheat, which is ground into semolina and mixed with water to produce the pasta dough. There is a vast choice of pasta shapes available and manufacturers are constantly devising new ones. A visit to your local Italian food shop will leave you spoilt for choice.

Fresh pasta is made from flour and eggs and is becoming increasingly easy to buy from supermarkets and delicatessens. It cooks very quickly, so care must be taken to avoid overcooking. Homemade pasta is cooked in seconds and has a wonderfully light melting texture. A pasta machine takes the hard work out of pasta making and produces excellent results.

Pasta is simple and foolproof to cook if you follow a few basic rules. Pasta needs to be cooked in abundant water so use a large pan, preferably high-sided. You need about 1 litre (1¾ pints) water per 125 g (4 oz) pasta, or 4 litres (7 pints) water to every 500 g (1 lb) pasta. Add ½-1 tablespoon salt and bring the water to a rolling boil. Add the pasta all at once. Spaghetti and other long pasta should be coiled around in the pan as it softens. Stir the pasta once to prevent it sticking, then return it quickly to the boil, covering the pan briefly. Boil the pasta until it is 'al dente', which means firm to the bite. Pasta should never be soft and mushy; it should retain some texture. Cooking times depend on the size and shape, but dried pasta takes between 6 and 12 minutes to cook. Don't adhere vehemently to the pack instructions – test frequently during the latter stages of cooking. Have your sauce and serving bowls warmed, so that you can drain the pasta and serve it immediately.

Many of the recipes in this book can be made in the time it takes to boil the water and cook your pasta. Even the most inexperienced cook will find them easy to follow, with perfect results every time.

Most of these recipes are substantial enough to be served as light suppers, with a salad or other accompaniment. There are no hard and fast rules as to whether individual recipes should be served as starters, snacks, suppers, or main courses – the choice is up to you. Of course, the quantities can easily be doubled up for feeding hungry hoards. Whatever your tastes or cooking needs, I am sure you will find plenty of inspiring pasta recipes to add to your repertoire.

HOMEMADE PASTA & SIMPLE SAUCES

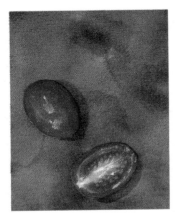

Turn to this section when time is really pressing and you will find a sauce you can put together in minutes. Pasta with sage and Parmesan is a classic which is always satisfying. Quick pesto is whizzed up in the food processor in minutes and fresh tomato sauce is the one to make when home-grown tomatoes are seasonal and cheap. At the beginning of this chapter you will find instructions for making your own pasta. It is well worth trying as the flavour is quite superb and it's not as time-consuming to prepare as you might think.

CONTENTS

HOMEMADE PASTA

MAKES ABOUT 350 G (12 OZ)

The flavour and texture of homemade pasta is incomparable. Making pasta is a skill that takes a little practice, but you will find it easy, once you get the hang of it. Consider investing in a pasta machine, to avoid rolling and cutting the pasta yourself. You will find it quick and simple to use. If you are not using a machine, make sure you roll out the dough as thinly as possible.

250 g (8 oz) strong white bread flour
½ teaspoon salt
2 eggs, beaten
1 tablespoon olive oil

1 Sift the flour and salt on to a work surface. Make a well in the centre and add the eggs and oil. Gradually draw the flour into the eggs, using your hands, until you have a soft dough.

2 Knead the dough on a lightly floured surface for 10 minutes until smooth and silky, then wrap in foil or cling film and leave to rest for 1 hour.

3 Put the dough through your chosen setting on the pasta machine, sprinkling the shaped pasta lightly with flour to stop it becoming sticky. Alternatively, roll out the dough as thinly as possible. Cut into shapes or roll up like a Swiss roll and slice to form strips of tagliatelle.

4 Cook the pasta without delay in plenty of boiling salted water for 2-5 minutes, depending on size, until tender. Drain and serve immediately.

VARIATIONS Flavoured pastas are easy to make and particularly delicious. Serve with simple sauces.

Spinach pasta Defrost 50 g (2 oz) frozen chopped spinach, then place in a sieve and press out as much water as possible. Add the spinach to the flour with the eggs and oil. You may need to add a little extra flour if the dough feels sticky.

Red pepper pasta Grill a medium-sized red pepper, turning occasionally, until charred. When cool enough to handle, peel off the skin and discard the core and seeds. Chop the pepper roughly, then place in a food processor or blender and work to a smooth paste. Add to the flour with the eggs and oil, adding more flour if the dough seems sticky.

Basil & Parmesan pasta Add 4 tablespoons finely chopped basil and 25 g (1 oz) freshly grated Parmesan to the flour with the eggs and oil.

RIGHT: HOMEMADE SPINACH PASTA, RED PEPPER PASTA AND PLAIN EGG PASTA

HERB SAUCE

SERVES 4

The herbs I have used can be varied to taste. Tossed with tagliatelle or pasta shapes, this makes a good accompaniment to meat or game.

25 g (1 oz) butter
1 teaspoon chopped thyme
1 teaspoon chopped marjoram
3 tablespoons single cream
2 tablespoons chopped parsley
salt and pepper to taste

1. Melt the butter in a small pan, add the thyme and marjoram and stir briefly. Add the cream, parsley and seasoning. Heat through gently; do not allow to boil.

GARLIC & CHILLI SAUCE

SERVES 4

Serve this sauce on spaghetti as the Italians do, or use it to spice up stuffed pasta.

4 tablespoons olive oil
2 cloves garlic, finely chopped
1 red chilli, seeded and finely chopped
salt and pepper to taste
2 tablespoons chopped parsley

1. Heat the oil in a small pan, add the garlic and cook for 2-3 minutes, until softened. Add the chilli and fry for 2 minutes, until the garlic is lightly browned. Add seasoning and parsley, and cook for 1 minute.

SAGE & PARMESAN SAUCE

SERVES 4

Serve this wonderful sauce spooned over any plain or stuffed pasta.

50 g (2 oz) butter
16 sage leaves, torn
salt and pepper to taste
2 tablespoons freshly grated Parmesan cheese

1. Place the butter, sage and seasoning in a small pan and heat gently, stirring. Serve sprinkled with Parmesan.

QUICK PESTO

SERVES 4-6

Pesto is worth making yourself when basil is available in abundance, and that really means growing it yourself. Store pesto in small jars covered with a layer of olive oil.

25 g (1 oz) toasted pine nuts
50 g (2 oz) fresh basil leaves
3 cloves garlic, finely chopped
salt to taste
6-8 tablespoons extra virgin olive oil
25 g (1 oz) Pecorino cheese, grated
50 g (2 oz) Parmesan cheese, grated

1. Finely chop the pine nuts in a blender or clean coffee grinder; then remove. Add the basil, garlic, salt and half the oil to the blender and work until smooth. Add the cheeses and remaining oil and blend until smooth, then add the pine nuts.

ABOVE: HERB SAUCE, GARLIC & CHILLI SAUCE   *CENTRE:* SAGE & PARMESAN SAUCE   *BELOW:* QUICK PESTO

TOMATO CREAM SAUCE

SERVES 4

It's amazing how just a little touch of cream can make this simple sauce really special. Combine it with your favourite pasta for a simple supper, or add a few torn basil leaves and serve it on fresh pasta for an elegant quick starter.

25 g (1 oz) butter
1 small onion, chopped
1 small carrot, chopped
1 stick celery, chopped
397 g (14 oz) can tomatoes
½ teaspoon sugar
salt and pepper to taste
2 tablespoons double cream
2 tablespoons freshly grated Parmesan cheese
basil leaves to garnish

1 Place all the ingredients, except the cream and Parmesan, in a saucepan and bring to the boil. Lower the heat and simmer, uncovered, for about 20 minutes until thickened.

2 Transfer the sauce to a blender or food processor and purée until smooth. Return to the pan, add the cream and reheat gently. Taste and add more seasoning if necessary.

3 Serve sprinkled with Parmesan and garnished with basil leaves.

TWO MUSHROOM SAUCE

SERVES 4

Dried porcini mushrooms are available in small sachets from most delicatessens. They give this sauce a deliciously intense flavour – perfect for pasta.

15 g (½ oz) dried porcini mushrooms
1 tablespoon olive oil
1 red onion, finely chopped
1 clove garlic, chopped
350 g (12 oz) chestnut mushrooms, sliced
1 teaspoon chopped oregano
1 tablespoon tomato purée
2 teaspoons lemon juice
salt and pepper to taste
oregano leaves to garnish

1 Place the porcini in a small bowl and cover with about 150 ml (¼ pint) boiling water. Leave to soak for 30 minutes, then drain; strain the liquid and reserve. Slice the mushrooms thinly.

2 Heat the oil in a saucepan, add the onion and fry for 3-4 minutes, until softened. Add the garlic, porcini and fresh mushrooms and cook for a few minutes, stirring occasionally.

3 Add the reserved liquid, oregano, tomato purée, lemon juice, salt and pepper. Bring to the boil, lower the heat and simmer, uncovered, for 20 minutes.

4 Serve sprinkled with oregano leaves.

FRESH TOMATO SAUCE

SERVES 4

This sauce is only as good as the tomatoes you use, so check for flavour before cooking with them. Organic and plum tomatoes are usually reliable.

500 g (1 lb) tomatoes
1 tablespoon olive oil
1 onion, chopped
1 clove garlic, chopped
bouquet garni
1 teaspoon sugar
salt and pepper to taste

1 To skin the tomatoes, hold on a fork over a gas flame turning until the skin blisters; or immerse in boiling water for about 2 minutes, then drain. Peel off the skins, then chop the tomatoes.

2 Heat the oil in a small saucepan, add the onion and fry for 2-3 minutes, until softened. Add all the remaining ingredients and bring to the boil. Lower the heat and simmer, uncovered, for 10 minutes until thickened and pulpy. Discard the bouquet garni before serving.

NOTE:
If you prefer a smoother sauce, purée in a blender or food processor before using.

PINE NUT & CHIVE SAUCE

SERVES 4

A subtle sauce to serve with any stuffed pasta, but particularly good with ravioli.

50 g (2 oz) pine nuts, toasted
150 ml (¼ pint) single cream
2 tablespoons snipped chives
salt and pepper to taste
1 tablespoon freshly grated Parmesan cheese

1 Place half the nuts in a small pan with the cream, half the chives and seasoning. Heat gently, stirring all the time; do not boil. Stir in the Parmesan.

2 Serve sprinkled with the remaining nuts and chives.

PROSCIUTTO CREAM SAUCE

SERVES 4

Prosciutto might be expensive, but a little goes a long way. This sauce is ideal with green pasta.

15 g (½ oz) unsalted butter
25 g (1 oz) prosciutto, diced
150 ml (¼ pint) single cream
salt and pepper to taste
freshly grated nutmeg to taste
freshly grated Parmesan to serve

1 Melt the butter in a pan, add the prosciutto and fry gently for 2-3 minutes, until lightly browned. Stir in the cream and heat gently; do not boil.

2 Add pepper and nutmeg; add salt if necessary. Serve sprinkled with Parmesan.

ABOVE: FRESH TOMATO SAUCE, PINE NUT & CHIVE SAUCE *BELOW*: PROSCIUTTO CREAM SAUCE

VEGETARIAN PASTA

Vegetarians need never feel they are missing out when it comes to pasta. There are so many flavoursome and colourful vegetables suitable for pasta sauces – the choice is endless. Make rich vegetable soups studded with tiny pasta shapes for a substantial snack, or rustle up a colourful tomato sauce laced with strips of grilled pepper for a quick supper dish. When entertaining, try serving a richly flavoured mushroom lasagne, or lasagne parcels stuffed with mascarpone and vegetables, and you may sway even the most hardened carnivore. Wholewheat pasta can be used for most of the recipes in this chapter if you prefer.

CONTENTS

RIGATONI WITH PEPPER & GARLIC SAUCE

SERVES 4

Peppers and garlic seem to have a natural affinity, and their sweet flavours are particularly good with pasta. The sauce can be made a couple of hours ahead of time if convenient.

1 red pepper
1 yellow pepper
1 green pepper
250-350 g (8-12 oz) rigatoni
4 tablespoons olive oil
3 cloves garlic, thinly sliced
1 tablespoon balsamic vinegar
salt and pepper to taste
2 tablespoons chopped parsley

1 Grill the peppers, turning occasionally, until the skins are charred. When cool enough to handle, peel off the skins. Halve the peppers, discard the seeds, then cut the flesh into thin slices.

2 Bring a large saucepan of salted water to the boil. Add the pasta, stir once and boil for 10-12 minutes until tender.

3 Meanwhile make the sauce. Heat 2 tablespoons of the oil in a pan, add the garlic and fry until softened and lightly browned. Add the remaining oil, vinegar, pepper slices, seasoning and parsley and heat through.

4 Drain the pasta and toss together with the sauce. Serve immediately.

PEPPERS STUFFED WITH ORZO

SERVES 4

Skinning the peppers before stuffing brings out their sweet taste. Orzo, or puntalette, are tiny pasta shaped like rice grains. They really absorb the flavours.

4 large peppers
250 g (8 oz) orzo
125 g (4 oz) stoned black olives, chopped
1 clove garlic, chopped
1 chilli, seeded and chopped
1 tablespoon capers, chopped
3 tablespoons chopped parsley
4 tablespoons extra virgin olive oil
salt and pepper to taste
2 tablespoons breadcrumbs
chilli slices to garnish

1 Preheat grill to high. Halve the peppers and discard the seeds. Grill, skin side up, until charred, then cool slightly and peel off the skins.

2 Meanwhile bring a large pan of salted water to the boil. Add the orzo, stir once and boil for 6-8 minutes until tender. Drain well.

3 Mix together the olives, garlic, chilli, capers and half of the parsley. Add the oil, orzo and seasoning; mix well.

4 Lay the peppers in an oiled shallow ovenproof dish and fill with the stuffing. Sprinkle with the breadcrumbs and remaining parsley.

5 Place under a moderate grill for 5-6 minutes, until the topping is crisp and the peppers are heated through. Garnish with chilli slices to serve.

ABOVE: RIGATONI WITH PEPPER & GARLIC SAUCE *BELOW*: PEPPERS STUFFED WITH ORZO

FETTUCINE WITH SUMMER VEGETABLES

SERVES 4

Use the first tender summer vegetables to make this delicate pasta dish.

25 g (1 oz) butter
1 tablespoon sunflower oil
1 clove garlic, chopped
175 g (6 oz) courgettes, cut into sticks
125 g (4 oz) thin asparagus, in pieces
125 g (4 oz) baby carrots
*175 g (6 oz) tomatoes, skinned, seeded and
    quartered*
125 ml (4 fl oz) dry white wine
1 tablespoon lemon juice
salt and pepper to taste
250-350 g (8-12 oz) fettucine
125 g (4 oz) mangetout or sugar snap peas
3 tablespoons double cream
freshly grated Parmesan cheese to serve

1 Heat the butter and oil in a saucepan, add the garlic and fry briefly. Add the courgettes, asparagus, carrots and tomatoes and cook for 5 minutes, stirring occasionally. Add the wine, lemon juice and seasoning. Bring to the boil, cover and cook gently for 10 minutes.

2 Meanwhile, bring a large saucepan of salted water to the boil. Add the fettucine, stir once and boil for 8 minutes. Add the mangetout and cook for 1 minute. Stir in the cream and warm through.

3 Drain the pasta, toss with the sauce and serve with grated Parmesan.

LASAGNE PARCELS WITH SPRING VEGETABLES

SERVES 4

500 g (1 lb) spinach
1 courgette, grated
1 carrot, grated
125 g (4 oz) ricotta or curd cheese
125 g (4 oz) mascarpone or cream cheese
4 tablespoons freshly grated Parmesan cheese
1 egg, beaten
salt and pepper to taste
freshly grated nutmeg to taste
250 g (8 oz) fresh lasagne
150 ml (¼ pint) single cream
150 ml (¼ pint) milk
25 g (1 oz) butter
parsley sprigs and lemon slices to garnish

1 Preheat the oven to 180°C (350°F/Gas 4). Place the spinach in a saucepan with just the water clinging to the leaves after washing and cook, covered for 5 minutes, until tender. Drain well and chop finely.

2 In a bowl, mix together the spinach, courgette, carrot, ricotta, mascarpone, 2 tablespoons Parmesan, the egg, seasoning and nutmeg.

3 Spread a little filling over each sheet of lasagne, then tuck in the ends and roll up like a parcel. Place in a single layer in a buttered shallow ovenproof dish.

4 Heat together the cream and milk and pour evenly over the lasagne. Dot with butter and sprinkle with the remaining Parmesan. Bake, uncovered, for 30 minutes, until golden brown. Garnish with parsley and lemon slices. Serve with a salad.

ABOVE: FETTUCINE WITH SUMMER VEGETABLES   *BELOW:* LASAGNE PARCELS WITH SPRING VEGETABLES

NOODLES WITH STIR-FRIED VEGETABLES

SERVES 4

Once the preparation is done, this dish is assembled in minutes.

250 g (8 oz) Chinese egg noodles
2 teaspoons sesame oil
2 tablespoons sunflower oil
1 clove garlic, chopped
1 leek, thinly sliced
227 g (8 oz) can water chestnuts, drained
½ red pepper, cored, seeded and chopped
175 g (6 oz) broccoli florets
1 teaspoon chilli bean sauce
2 teaspoons tomato purée
2 tablespoons dry sherry
2 tablespoons soy sauce
½ teaspoon sugar
125 g (4 oz) oyster mushrooms

1 Bring a large pan of salted water to the boil. Add the noodles, cover, remove from the heat and leave to stand for 6 minutes. Drain and toss in sesame oil.

2 Heat the sunflower oil in a large frying pan or wok. Add the garlic and leek and stir-fry for 1 minute. Add the sliced water chestnuts, pepper and broccoli and stir-fry for 1 minute.

3 Mix together the chilli bean sauce, tomato purée, sherry, soy sauce, sugar and 2 tablespoons water. Add to the pan and stir well. Cover and simmer for 2-3 minutes.

4 Stir in the noodles and mushrooms. Cover and cook for 2 minutes. Serve immediately.

BOWS WITH TOMATO & PEPPER SAUCE

SERVES 4

Illustrated on back cover.

1 yellow pepper
2 tablespoons olive oil
1 onion, sliced
397 g (14 oz) can chopped tomatoes
1 tablespoon tomato purée
salt and pepper to taste
250-350 g (8-12 oz) pasta bows
50 g (2 oz) black olives
handful of basil leaves, torn if large
freshly grated Parmesan cheese to serve

1 Preheat the grill to high. Grill the pepper until the skin is charred, turning occasionally. When cool enough to handle, peel off the skin, discard the seeds and slice the flesh.

2 Heat the oil in a saucepan, add the onion and fry until softened. Add the tomatoes, tomato purée, yellow pepper, salt and pepper. Bring to the boil, then simmer for 15 minutes, until pulpy.

3 Meanwhile cook the pasta. Bring a large saucepan of salted water to the boil. Add the pasta, stir once and boil for 10-12 minutes until tender.

4 Stir the olives and basil into the sauce.

5 Drain the pasta and transfer to warmed serving plates. Pour the sauce over the top and serve with Parmesan.

RIGHT: NOODLES WITH STIR-FRIED VEGETABLES

MUSHROOM LASAGNE

SERVES 4-6

15 g (½ oz) dried porcini mushrooms
2 tablespoons olive oil
2 shallots, chopped
1 tablespoon tomato purée
2 tablespoons chopped parsley
salt and pepper to taste
500 g (1 lb) chestnut mushrooms, sliced
600 ml (1 pint) milk
40 g (1½ oz) butter
40 g (1½ oz) plain flour
250-300 g (8-10 oz) fresh lasagne
50 g (2 oz) freshly grated Parmesan cheese

1 Soak the porcini in 300 ml (½ pint) hot water for 30 minutes then drain; strain the soaking liquid and reserve. Slice the mushrooms thinly.

2 Preheat oven to 200°C (400°F/Gas 6). Heat the oil in a pan and fry the shallots until softened. Add the porcini, reserved liquid, tomato purée, parsley and seasoning. Simmer for 15 minutes, then add the fresh mushrooms and cook for 5 minutes.

3 Warm the milk. Melt the butter in a pan, add the flour and cook for 1 minute. Whisk in the milk then cook, whisking, until the sauce is smooth and thickened. Add seasoning.

4 Layer the ingredients in a buttered shallow oblong dish in the following order: sauce, lasagne, mushroom, lasagne, mushroom, lasagne, sauce; sprinkling Parmesan over each layer. Bake for 15-20 minutes, until golden brown. Serve with a salad.

RIGATONI FIORENTINA

SERVES 4

This dish is similar to one served at my favourite Italian café.

1 quantity fresh tomato sauce (page 14)
salt and pepper to taste
250 g (8 oz) rigatoni
125 g (4 oz) spinach leaves
50 g (2 oz) gruyère cheese, grated
2 tablespoons freshly grated Parmesan cheese
1 tablespoon olive oil

1 Make the tomato sauce and keep warm. Bring a large saucepan of salted water to the boil. Add the pasta, stir once and boil for 10-12 minutes until tender.

2 Meanwhile cook the spinach in the minimum of water for about 5 minutes, until tender. Drain thoroughly and chop roughly. Stir into the tomato sauce.

3 Preheat the grill to high. Drain the rigatoni, add to the sauce and mix well. Transfer to a warmed oiled ovenproof dish. Sprinkle with the gruyère and Parmesan and drizzle with the oil. Place under the hot grill for 2-3 minutes, until golden and bubbling. Serve immediately.

ORECCHIETTE WITH SWISS CHARD

SERVES 4

Small ear-shaped orecchiette have a wonderful firm texture as they are made from durum semolina. They are particularly good with vegetable sauces. When Swiss chard is out of season, use spinach leaves instead.

250 g (8 oz) Swiss chard, stalks removed
250 g (8 oz) orecchiette
4 tablespoons olive oil
1 red chilli, seeded and chopped
3 cloves garlic, finely chopped
salt and pepper to taste

1 Rinse the chard, drain thoroughly and shred.

2 Bring a large saucepan of salted water to the boil. Add the orecchiette, stir once and boil for 5 minutes. Add the chard and cook for a further 6-7 minutes until the pasta is tender.

3 Meanwhile make the sauce. Heat half of the oil in a small pan. Add the chilli and garlic and fry for 2-3 minutes, until lightly browned. Add the remaining oil and warm through.

4 Drain the pasta and chard thoroughly. Transfer to serving bowls and spoon the chilli and garlic sauce on top to serve.

SPINACH GNOCCHI WITH TOMATO SAUCE

SERVES 4

250 g (8 oz) frozen chopped spinach, defrosted
25 g (1 oz) butter
1 shallot, finely chopped
125 g (4 oz) ricotta or curd cheese
2 egg yolks
75 g (3 oz) plain flour
50 g (2 oz) Parmesan, freshly grated
freshly grated nutmeg to taste
salt and pepper to taste
1 quantity Tomato Cream Sauce (page 12)
freshly grated Parmesan to serve

1 Place the spinach in a fine sieve and press out as much water as possible, then transfer to a bowl.

2 Melt the butter in a pan, add the shallot and fry gently for 2-3 minutes, until softened. Add to the spinach with the ricotta, egg yolks, flour, Parmesan, nutmeg and seasoning. Mix thoroughly to a smooth dough. Cover and chill for 20 minutes until firm.

3 To shape the gnocchi, break off small pieces of dough and form into balls. Bring a large pan of salted water to the boil, then reduce to a simmer and add the gnocchi. Cook, uncovered, for about 5 minutes until they rise to the surface.

4 Using a slotted spoon, transfer the gnocchi to warmed serving bowls and pour over the tomato cream sauce. Sprinkle with Parmesan to serve.

ABOVE: ORECCHIETTE WITH SWISS CHARD *BELOW*: SPINACH GNOCCHI WITH TOMATO SAUCE

SPAGHETTI WITH WALNUT & PARSLEY SAUCE

SERVES 4

This is an English version of pesto, using easily available ingredients. Wholemeal spaghetti is very good with this sauce.

25 g (1 oz) shelled walnuts
1 clove garlic, crushed
15 g (½ oz) parsley
3 tablespoons freshly grated Parmesan cheese
150 ml (¼ pint) extra virgin olive oil
salt and pepper to taste
250-350 g (8-12 oz) spaghetti
parsley sprigs to garnish

1 Place the walnuts, garlic and parsley in a blender or clean coffee grinder and chop finely. Add the Parmesan and mix well. Gradually add the oil until well blended. Taste and season with salt and pepper.

2 Bring a large saucepan of salted water to the boil. Add the spaghetti, stir once and boil for 10-12 minutes until tender. Drain and return to the pan. And the sauce and warm through, stirring well. Serve immediately, garnished with parsley.

TRENETTE WITH FRENCH BEANS & PESTO

SERVES 4

You need to use fresh pesto for this recipe; see page 10 for a quick version. If trenette is not available use tagliatelle instead.

250 g (8 oz) French beans, cut into short lengths
salt and pepper to taste
250-350 g (8-12 oz) fresh trenette
4 tablespoons pesto
2 tablespoons olive oil
freshly shredded Parmesan to serve
basil leaves to garnish

1 Cook the French beans in a large saucepan containing plenty of boiling salted water for 10 minutes. Add the pasta, return to the boil and cook for 2-3 minutes until the pasta is tender.

2 Meanwhile warm the pesto with the oil in a small saucepan. Drain the pasta, adding 3-4 tablespoons of the cooking liquid to the pesto.

3 Toss the pasta with the pesto and serve sprinkled with Parmesan and freshly ground pepper. Garnish with basil leaves.

ABOVE: SPAGHETTI WITH WALNUT & PARSLEY SAUCE   *BELOW*: TRENETTE WITH FRENCH BEANS & PESTO

PASTA TWISTS WITH FENNEL SAUCE

SERVES 4

A dash of Pernod brings out the subtle aniseed flavour of the fennel. The sauce can be made several hours before serving; it also freezes well.

25 g (1 oz) butter
1 onion, chopped
250 g (8 oz) fennel bulb
1 tablespoon Pernod
150 ml (¼ pint) white wine
150 ml (¼ pint) vegetable stock
250 g (8 oz) pasta twists
2 tablespoons single cream
salt and pepper to taste

1 Melt the butter in a small pan, add the onion and fry until softened, about 5 minutes. Meanwhile trim off the leaves from the fennel and reserve. Slice the bulb finely.

2 Add the sliced fennel to the pan, stirring well. Add the Pernod, wine and stock and bring to the boil. Cover and simmer for 15 minutes until the fennel is tender.

3 Meanwhile cook the pasta. Bring a large saucepan of salted water to the boil. Add the pasta, stir once and boil for 10-12 minutes until tender.

4 Put half of the sauce in a food processor or blender and work until fairly smooth. Return to the pan. Stir in the remaining sauce and cream. Warm through and check seasoning.

5 Drain the pasta and toss with the sauce. Serve sprinkled with the fennel leaves.

PAPPARDELLE WITH RICH MUSHROOM SAUCE

SERVES 4

Pappardelle are very wide flat noodles, which sometimes have wavy edges. You can use tagliatelle instead, but reduce the boiling time to 10-12 minutes.

1 tablespoon olive oil
2 shallots, chopped
1 clove garlic, chopped
2 rashers back bacon, chopped
250 g (8 oz) chestnut mushrooms, sliced
150 ml (¼ pint) canned consommé
3 tablespoons madeira
salt and pepper to taste
250-350 g (8-12 oz) pappardelle
2 tablespoons double cream

1 Heat the oil in a saucepan, add the shallots, garlic and bacon and fry until softened, about 5 minutes. Add the mushrooms and stir well.

2 Add the consommé, madeira and seasoning. Bring to the boil and simmer uncovered for 15 minutes, stirring occasionally.

3 Bring a large saucepan of salted water to the boil. Add the pasta, stir once and boil for 10-12 minutes until tender. Drain well.

4 Stir the cream into the sauce and pour over the pasta. Toss well to serve.

RICH VEGETABLE SOUP

SERVES 4-6

To prepare the vegetables instantly, put them all in the food processor and work the machine until they are evenly chopped.

1.5 litres (2½ pints) vegetable stock
4 carrots, finely chopped
2 leeks, finely chopped
3 sticks celery, finely chopped
2 potatoes, finely chopped
¼ green cabbage, shredded
125 g (4 oz) French beans, chopped
bouquet garni
salt and pepper to taste
50 g (2 oz) tiny pasta shapes

1 Pour the stock into a large saucepan. Add all of the vegetables, the bouquet garni, salt and pepper. Bring to the boil, cover and simmer for 20 minutes, stirring occasionally.

2 Add the pasta and simmer for a further 10 minutes.

3 Serve this hearty soup with lots of warm bread.

PASTA & CHICK PEA SOUP

SERVES 4

A substantial, tasty soup – perfect for winter. The basic soup can be made in advance, but add the pasta shortly before serving otherwise it will become too soft.

---

2 tablespoons olive oil
2 cloves garlic, chopped
1 onion, chopped
1 carrot, chopped
1 stick celery, chopped
397 g (14 oz) can tomatoes
1 tablespoon tomato purée
900 ml (1½ pints) vegetable stock
2 rosemary sprigs
salt and pepper to taste
397 g (14 oz) can chick peas, drained
75 g (3 oz) tiny pasta shapes
2 teaspoons pesto

1 Heat the oil in a large saucepan. Add the garlic, onion, carrot and celery. Stir well, cover and cook gently for 5 minutes. Add the tomatoes, tomato purée, stock, rosemary, salt and pepper. Bring to the boil, cover and simmer for 10 minutes.

2 Add the chick peas and pasta and cook for a further 10-12 minutes, until the pasta is tender.

3 Stir in the pesto just before serving.

PASTA SALADS

Pasta salads are ideal for light meals, especially in summer. They can be a meal in themselves or provide an interesting side dish to serve with fish, meat or barbecued foods. Give full rein to your imagination by selecting interesting pasta shapes, such as three colour spirals, knots or wholewheat shells. Dressings for pasta salads need plenty of punch. Choose from a garlicy mayonnaise, a walnut and mustard dressing or a Mexican-style blend of tomatoes, chillies and coriander. Take extra care to avoid overcooking the pasta, cooling it quickly under running cold water to preserve its bite. Many of these salads can happily be made several hours before you serve them.

CONTENTS

PASTA, WATERCRESS & CASHEW NUT SALAD

SERVES 4-6

This simple fresh-tasting salad is delicious served with cold meats, or barbecued food.

175 g (6 oz) pasta shells
1 bunch of watercress
125 g (4 oz) cashew nuts
1 red pepper, cored, seeded and diced

DRESSING
2 tablespoons walnut oil
1 tablespoon wine vinegar
2 teaspoons Dijon mustard
1 tablespoon snipped chives
salt and pepper to taste

1 Bring a large saucepan of salted water to the boil. Add the pasta shells, stir once and boil for 10-12 minutes until tender. Drain, then refresh under cold water and drain thoroughly. Toss in a little oil to prevent sticking.

2 Place the pasta in a serving bowl. Roughly chop the watercress, then add to the pasta with the nuts and red pepper; mix lightly.

3 Place all the dressing ingredients in a small bowl and whisk together with a fork. Pour over the salad and toss lightly just before serving.

TRICOLORE SALAD

SERVES 4-6

Capture all the flavours of summer with this colourful salad. Use *amori* (pasta knots) or spirals.

250 g (8 oz) pasta knots or spirals
1 ripe avocado
lemon juice for sprinkling
250 g (8 oz) cherry tomatoes, quartered
125 g (4 oz) mozzarella cheese, diced
handful of basil leaves, shredded if large

DRESSING
1 tablespoon mayonnaise
2 tablespoons olive oil
1 tablespoon wine vinegar
1 teaspoon sugar
1 clove garlic, crushed
salt and pepper to taste

1 Bring a large saucepan of salted water to the boil. Add the pasta, stir once and boil for 10-12 minutes until tender. Drain, then refresh under cold water and drain thoroughly. Toss in a little oil to prevent sticking.

2 Place the pasta in a bowl. Peel, stone and dice the avocado. Toss in a little lemon juice to prevent discoloration. Add to the pasta with the tomatoes, mozzarella and basil.

3 Place the dressing ingredients in a small bowl and whisk together with a fork. Pour over the salad, toss lightly and serve immediately.

ABOVE: PASTA, WATERCRESS & CASHEW NUT SALAD   *BELOW:* TRICOLORE SALAD

MEXICAN TOMATO SALAD

SERVES 4-6

The dressing for this salad can be made up to a day in advance, as the flavours improve with keeping. Do not mix until just before serving, otherwise the pasta will soften as it absorbs the dressing on standing.

250 g (8 oz) tricolour pasta spirals
1/4 Spanish onion, chopped
250 g (8 oz) ripe tomatoes, chopped
1/2 green chilli, seeded and chopped
3 tablespoons chopped coriander leaves
juice of 2 limes
4 sun-dried tomatoes
salt and pepper to taste
coriander leaves to garnish

1 Bring a large saucepan of salted water to the boil. Add the pasta, stir once and boil for 10-12 minutes until tender. Drain, then refresh under cold water. Drain well and toss in a little oil to prevent sticking.

2 Place the onion, tomatoes, chilli, coriander and lime juice in a food processor and blend until fairly smooth. Add one of the sun-dried tomatoes, with salt and pepper, and blend again briefly.

3 Just before serving toss the pasta in the dressing. Slice the remaining sun-dried tomatoes and sprinkle over the salad. Garnish with coriander leaves to serve.

PEPERONATA PASTA SALAD

SERVES 4-6

I love the sweet, slightly charred taste of grilled peppers. Serve this as a starter or accompaniment to grilled food.

280 g (8 oz) chiocciole or pasta spirals
1 red pepper
1 yellow pepper
1 green pepper
2 tablespoons chopped spring onions

DRESSING
250 g (8 oz) tomatoes, skinned, seeded and
  chopped
2 tablespoons olive oil
1 tablespoon lemon juice
2 cloves garlic, chopped
1 teaspoon paprika
salt and pepper to taste

1 Bring a large saucepan of salted water to the boil. Add the pasta, stir once and boil for 10-12 minutes until tender. Drain, then refresh under cold water and drain thoroughly. Toss in a little oil to prevent sticking.

2 Preheat the grill to high and grill the peppers, turning occasionally, until their skins are charred. When cool enough to handle, peel off the skins. Halve the peppers, discard seeds and cut the flesh into thin strips. Place in a large bowl, with the pasta and spring onions. Mix lightly.

3 Place all the dressing ingredients in a food processor or blender and work until fairly smooth. Pour over the salad and toss lightly to serve.

ARTICHOKE & SALAMI SALAD

SERVES 4

The rustic flavour of this salad will appeal to those who like strong tastes. Don't be tempted to use a cheap alternative – only Italian salami will do.

175 g (6 oz) wholewheat pasta shells
425 g (15 oz) can artichoke hearts
50 g (2 oz) Italian salami
50 g (2 oz) black olives
75 g (3 oz) button mushrooms
½ red onion, thinly sliced

DRESSING
1 tablespoon balsamic vinegar
3 tablespoons extra virgin olive oil
salt and pepper to taste

1 Bring a large saucepan of salted water to the boil. Add the pasta, stir once and boil for 10-12 minutes until tender. Drain, then refresh under cold water and drain thoroughly. Toss in a little oil to prevent sticking.

2 Drain the artichokes thoroughly, then slice thinly. Cut the salami into strips, halve the olives and slice the mushrooms and onion. Place the pasta in a large bowl with the artichokes, salami, olives, mushrooms and onion.

3 Place the dressing ingredients in a screw-topped jar and shake well to mix. Pour over the salad and toss lightly to serve.

PRAWN & PASTA SALAD

SERVES 4-6

Serve this as a pretty summer starter, or as part of a buffet meal. Other seafood such as cooked mussels, clams or squid rings can be used instead of – or in addition to – the prawns.

175 g (6 oz) pipe rigate or pasta shells
1 small head fennel
2 spring onions, chopped
1 tablespoon chopped dill
125 g (4 oz) cherry tomatoes, halved
250 g (8 oz) peeled prawns
few unshelled cooked prawns (optional)

DRESSING
2 tablespoons olive oil
1 tablespoon lemon juice
1 clove garlic, crushed
2 teaspoons finely chopped root ginger
1 teaspoon coarse-grain mustard
1 teaspoon sugar
salt and pepper to taste

1 Bring a large saucepan of salted water to the boil. Add the pasta, stir once and boil for 10-12 minutes until tender. Drain, then refresh under cold water and drain well. Toss in a little oil to prevent sticking.

2 Quarter the fennel, remove the core, then slice thinly. Place in a large bowl with the pasta, spring onions, dill, tomatoes and peeled prawns. Mix well.

3 Place all the dressing ingredients in a small bowl and whisk with a fork. Pour over the salad just before serving. Garnish with whole cooked prawns if desired.

ABOVE: ARTICHOKE & SALAMI SALAD   *BELOW*: PRAWN & PASTA SALAD

BACON & FRIED PASTA SALAD

SERVES 4-6

Fried pasta has an interesting taste and texture. Tossed with crisp leaves, it makes a very attractive side salad.

125 g (4 oz) ondule or pasta spirals
2 tablespoons olive oil
125 g (4 oz) streaky bacon, chopped
50 g (2 oz) pine nuts
1 teaspoon finely chopped rosemary
1 clove garlic, chopped
2 tablespoons sherry vinegar
pepper to taste
1 small head frisée (curly endive)
1-2 tomatoes, sliced
15 g (½ oz) freshly shredded Parmesan cheese

1 Bring a large saucepan of salted water to the boil. Add the pasta, stir once and boil for 10-12 minutes until tender. Drain, then refresh under cold water and drain thoroughly. Toss in a little oil to prevent sticking.

2 Heat 1 tablespoon oil in a frying pan, add the bacon and fry for about 5 minutes, until crisp. Add the pasta and fry for a further 5 minutes, turning constantly, until the pasta starts to become crisp. Add the pine nuts, rosemary and garlic and fry for 2 minutes, stirring. Add the remaining oil, the vinegar and pepper. Warm through.

3 Line individual serving plates with frisée and a few tomato slices. Spoon the pasta on top and sprinkle with Parmesan to serve.

SMOKED CHICKEN & PASTA SALAD

SERVES 4-6

175 g (6 oz) pasta bows
½ cucumber
2 carrots
2 tablespoons olive oil
2 slices bread, cubed
250 g (8 oz) smoked chicken, cubed
1 lettuce, finely shredded
mint sprigs to garnish

DRESSING
2 tablespoons natural yogurt
2 tablespoons chopped mint
1 tablespoon wine vinegar
1 tablespoon olive oil
1 clove garlic, crushed
1 teaspoon clear honey
salt and pepper to taste

1 Bring a large pan of salted water to the boil. Add the pasta, stir once and boil for 10-12 minutes until tender. Drain, then refresh under cold water. Drain well and toss in a little oil to prevent sticking.

2 Cut the cucumber and carrots into thin sticks.

3 Heat the oil in a frying pan. Add the bread and fry until crisp and golden; drain on kitchen paper.

4 Place all the dressing ingredients in a bowl and whisk together with a fork.

5 Combine the pasta, chicken, cucumber and carrots in a serving bowl. Pour over the dressing and toss well. Serve on a bed of lettuce, sprinkled with the croûtons and garnished with mint.

PASTA WITH
CHEESE & EGGS

The simplest way to serve pasta is with a
knob of butter and a generous grating of
Parmesan cheese. Many other cheeses can be
used with pasta to delicious effect – try
creamy fontina, melting mozzarella and tangy
gorgonzola. When the cupboard is almost
bare, cheese and eggs make satisfying pasta
dishes with very little else. Eggs stirred into a
tomato sauce make it rich and creamy, while
fontina cheese sauce gives a welcome sharp
edge to morsels of gnocchi. For an indulgent
starter, try serving pasta bows with gorgonzola
and pistachio sauce.

CONTENTS

PENNE WITH FONTINA & TARRAGON SAUCE

SERVES 4

Fontina cheese is used in Italy to make fonduta – the Italian version of a fondue. It melts very easily and has a creamy taste with a sharp tang. Add some lightly cooked sliced mushrooms before serving, if you like.

250-350 g (8-12 oz) penne
150 ml (¼ pint) milk
125 g (4 oz) fontina cheese, cubed
1 egg yolk
1 tablespoon tarragon leaves
salt and pepper to taste
tarragon sprigs to garnish
freshly grated Parmesan cheese to serve

1 Bring a large saucepan of salted water to the boil. Add the pasta, stir once and boil for 10-12 minutes until tender.

2 Meanwhile make the sauce. Warm the milk, then pour into a small bowl over a pan of simmering water. Add the cheese and egg yolk and cook, stirring occasionally, until the sauce is smooth. Do not overheat or the egg will curdle. Stir in the tarragon and pepper. Taste and add salt if necessary.

3 Drain the pasta and mix with the sauce. Transfer to individual bowls. Garnish with tarragon and sprinkle with Parmesan and pepper to serve.

PASTA WHEELS WITH MASCARPONE & PECAN SAUCE

SERVES 4

Mascarpone is a fresh Italian cream cheese sold in tubs. Substitute cream cheese or curd cheese if you can't find it.

250-350 g (8-12 oz) pasta wheels
125 g (4 oz) mascarpone cheese
150 ml (¼ pint) single cream
1 tablespoon freshly grated Parmesan cheese
salt and pepper to taste
1 teaspoon chopped marjoram
a little milk (optional)
1 tablespoon olive oil
1 tablespoon lemon juice
25 g (1 oz) shelled pecan nuts, chopped
marjoram sprigs to garnish

1 Bring a large saucepan of salted water to the boil. Add the pasta, stir once and boil for 10-12 minutes until tender.

2 Meanwhile make the sauce. Heat the mascarpone gently in a small saucepan until melted. Add the cream, Parmesan, salt, pepper and marjoram and heat through gently. Add a little milk if the sauce seems too thick.

3 Drain the pasta and toss in the oil and lemon juice. Divide the pasta between warmed plates and pour over the sauce. Sprinkle with nuts and marjoram. Serve immediately.

ABOVE: PENNE WITH FONTINA & TARRAGON SAUCE *BELOW*: PASTA WITH MASCARPONE & PECAN SAUCE

CHEESY AUBERGINE PASTA PIE

SERVES 4

This dish can be assembled several hours in advance – ready to bake when needed. It is perfect for vegetarians.

500 g (1 lb) aubergines, thinly sliced
3-4 tablespoons olive oil
salt and pepper to taste
175 g (6 oz) pappardelle or fusilli
600 ml (1 pint) bottled tomato sauce
125 g (4 oz) mozzarella cheese, thinly sliced
2 tablespoons freshly grated Parmesan cheese

1 Preheat oven to 190°C (375°F/Gas 5) and preheat grill to medium high. Brush the aubergine slices with a little oil and sprinkle with salt. Grill for 3-4 minutes, until lightly browned then turn, brush again and brown the other side.

2 Bring a large pan of salted water to the boil. Add the pasta, stir once and boil for 10-12 minutes until almost tender; drain well. Toss in a little oil to prevent sticking.

3 Arrange half of the aubergine slices over the base of a buttered ovenproof dish. Pour half of the tomato sauce over them. Spread the pasta over the sauce and arrange the mozzarella on top. Sprinkle with a little of the Parmesan.

4 Cover with the rest of the aubergine slices, then the remaining tomato sauce. Sprinkle with Parmesan and drizzle a little oil over the top. Bake for 30 minutes, until bubbling and golden brown.

SPAGHETTI WITH AUBERGINES & RICOTTA

SERVES 4

If possible, use the salted version of ricotta for this dish.

1 medium aubergine
salt and pepper to taste
250-350 g (8-12 oz) spaghetti
4 tablespoons olive oil
1 onion, chopped
2 cloves garlic, chopped
397 g (14 oz) can chopped tomatoes
125 g (4 oz) ricotta cheese
handful of basil or parsley leaves
freshly grated Parmesan cheese to serve

1 Cut the aubergine lengthwise into thin slices. Place in a colander, sprinkle with salt and leave for 30 minutes. Rinse and pat dry with kitchen paper.

2 Bring a large pan of salted water to the boil. Coil in the spaghetti, stir once and boil for 10-12 minutes until tender. Drain thoroughly.

3 Meanwhile heat half of the oil in a frying pan. When very hot, add the aubergine slices and stir-fry quickly until softened and lightly browned; remove.

4 Add the remaining oil to the pan and fry the onion until softened. Add the garlic, tomatoes, salt and pepper and bring to the boil. Simmer gently for 10 minutes, add the aubergine slices and cook gently for 2-3 minutes.

5 Put the spaghetti into a warm serving dish. Add the sauce and crumble in the ricotta. Toss gently and sprinkle with basil or parsley. Serve with freshly grated Parmesan.

ABOVE: CHEESY AUBERGINE PASTA PIE *BELOW:* SPAGHETTI WITH AUBERGINES & RICOTTA

GNOCCHI WITH FONTINA CHEESE

SERVES 4

Choose floury potatoes, such as desirée or wilja, for these light fluffy morsels. If you can't get fontina, use gruyère instead.

500 g (1 lb) medium potatoes
1 egg, beaten
150 g (5 oz) plain flour
2 teaspoons chopped thyme
salt and pepper to taste
175 g (6 oz) fontina cheese, grated
150 ml (¼ pint) milk
2 tablespoons freshly grated Parmesan cheese
thyme sprigs to garnish

1 Boil the potatoes in their skins until tender, about 20-25 minutes; drain. When cool enough to handle, peel off the skins and mash the potatoes. Add the egg, flour, thyme, salt and pepper; mix well.

2 Divide the dough in half and form each piece into a long sausage on a lightly floured surface. Cut into 2.5 cm (1 inch) lengths and roll each piece along the prongs of a fork to mark ridges.

3 Place the fontina and milk in a bowl over a pan of simmering water. Heat gently, stirring occasionally, until smooth. Remove pan from heat and keep the sauce warm over the hot water.

4 Bring a large pan of salted water to the boil. Add the gnocchi and boil for 4-5 minutes, until they float to the surface. Remove with a slotted spoon and divide between individual serving dishes. Pour the cheese sauce over the gnocchi and sprinkle with Parmesan. Serve immediately, garnished with thyme.

BOWS BAKED WITH HAM & EGGS

SERVES 4-6

For vegetarians replace the ham with par-cooked vegetables, such as mushrooms and broccoli.

250 g (8 oz) pasta bows
600 ml (1 pint) milk
40 g (1½ oz) butter
40 g (1½ oz) plain flour
2 eggs, beaten
freshly grated nutmeg
75 g (3 oz) gruyère cheese, grated
250 g (8 oz) cooked ham, chopped
salt and pepper to taste
2 tablespoons freshly grated Parmesan cheese

1 Preheat oven to 180°C (350°F/Gas 4). Bring a large saucepan of salted water to the boil. Add the pasta, stir once and boil for 10-12 minutes until just tender.

2 Meanwhile make the sauce. Warm the milk. Melt the butter in small pan, add the flour and cook for 1 minute. Whisk in the milk all at once, then cook, whisking, until the sauce is thickened and smooth. Simmer for 2 minutes. Remove from the heat and stir in the eggs, nutmeg, gruyère, ham, salt and pepper.

3 Drain the pasta and toss in a little oil to prevent sticking. Spread half in a buttered ovenproof dish and cover with half the sauce. Repeat the layers, then sprinkle with Parmesan. Bake for about 30 minutes, until bubbling and golden brown. Serve immediately.

ABOVE: GNOCCHI WITH FONTINA CHEESE *BELOW*: BOWS BAKED WITH HAM & EGGS

RIGATONI WITH TOMATO & EGG SAUCE

SERVES 4

Including eggs in this tomato sauce gives a rich, creamy texture and taste. A great spur of the moment meal, as you are likely to have the ingredients at home.

2 tablespoons olive oil
25 g (1 oz) butter
1 onion, chopped
397 g (14 oz) carton passata
salt and pepper to taste
350 g (12 oz) rigatoni
2 eggs, beaten
2 tablespoons freshly grated Parmesan cheese
10-12 basil leaves, torn if large

1 Heat the oil and butter in a pan, add the onion and fry gently for 5 minutes, until softened. Add the passata and seasoning. Bring to the boil and simmer, uncovered, for 12-15 minutes until thickened.

2 Meanwhile bring a large pan of salted water to the boil. Add the pasta, stir once and boil for 10-12 minutes until tender. Drain and return to the pan. Keep warm.

3 To finish the sauce, lower the heat to a gentle simmer, then slowly pour in the eggs, stirring all the time, until the sauce is thickened and creamy; do not allow to boil. Stir in half of the Parmesan and basil. Check seasoning.

4 Pour the sauce over the pasta. Sprinkle with the remaining Parmesan and basil to serve.

SHELLS WITH RICOTTA & TOMATO SAUCE

SERVES 4

These giant shells look most interesting nestling in their sauce. If time is really short, use one of the ready-made tomato sauces now available instead of making your own.

250 g (8 oz) large pasta shells
350 g (12 oz) ricotta cheese
1 egg, beaten
2 tablespoons chopped basil
3 tablespoons freshly grated Parmesan cheese
salt and pepper to taste
1 quantity fresh tomato sauce (page 14)
basil sprigs to garnish

1 Preheat oven to 180°C (350°F/Gas 4). Bring a large saucepan of salted water to the boil. Add the pasta, stir once and boil for 8 minutes; drain well.

2 Meanwhile, in a bowl mix together the ricotta, egg, basil, half of the Parmesan, salt and pepper.

3 Spoon the stuffing into the shells and arrange in a buttered shallow ovenproof dish. Pour the sauce over the shells and sprinkle with the remaining Parmesan. Bake for 25 minutes, until the topping is golden brown.

4 Serve immediately, garnished with basil.

BOWS WITH GORGONZOLA & PISTACHIO SAUCE

SERVES 4

This interesting combination of warm flavours makes a great starter on a cold day and it is certainly one of my favourites.

250-350 g (8-12 oz) pasta bows
50 g (2 oz) unsalted butter
125 g (4 oz) gorgonzola cheese, cubed
150 ml (¼ pint) single cream
1 tablespoon brandy
25 g (1 oz) shelled pistachio nuts, chopped
salt and pepper to taste

1 Bring a large saucepan of salted water to the boil. Add the pasta, stir once and boil for 10-12 minutes until tender. Drain well.

2 Meanwhile make the sauce. Chop up the butter and place it in a small pan with the cheese. Heat very gently until the cheese has melted, then add the cream and bring to a simmer, stirring lightly. Add the brandy and all but 1 tablespoon of the nuts. Heat through, taste and add pepper, and salt if necessary.

3 Divide the pasta between warmed serving plates. Pour the sauce over the pasta and sprinkle with pepper and the remaining nuts. Serve immediately.

SHELLS WITH THREE CHEESE SAUCE

SERVES 4

Serve this unashamedly rich pasta sauce with a salad of bitter leaves, such as frisée and radicchio.

350 g (12 oz) pasta shells
150 ml (¼ pint) single cream
75 g (3 oz) dolcelatte cheese, chopped
125 g (4 oz) mozzarella cheese, finely chopped
50 g (2 oz) freshly grated Parmesan cheese
25 g (1 oz) butter
1 tablespoon snipped chives
1 tablespoon chopped parsley
pepper to taste
parsley sprigs to garnish

1 Bring a large saucepan of salted water to the boil. Add the pasta, stir once and boil for 10-12 minutes until tender.

2 Preheat the grill to high. Drain the pasta well, then return to the pan. Add the cream, dolcelatte, mozzarella and half of the Parmesan. Stir in the butter, herbs and pepper and heat through gently until the cheeses are starting to melt.

3 Transfer the mixture to a warmed ovenproof serving dish and sprinkle with the remaining Parmesan. Place under the grill for a few minutes until golden brown. Serve immediately, garnished with parsley.

ABOVE: BOWS WITH GORGONZOLA & PISTACHIO SAUCE *BELOW*: SHELLS WITH THREE CHEESE SAUCE

CHEESE PASTA SOUFFLÉ

SERVES 4-6

Don't be nervous of making this soufflé – it is
virtually foolproof!

75 g (3 oz) pasta shells or twists
250 g (8 oz) spinach
50 g (2 oz) butter
125 g (4 oz) back bacon, chopped
50 g (2 oz) plain flour
450 ml (¾ pint) milk
3 eggs, separated
freshly grated nutmeg
75 g (3 oz) mature Cheddar cheese, grated
2 tablespoons freshly grated Parmesan cheese
salt and pepper to taste

1 Preheat oven to 190°C (375°F/Gas 5). Bring a
large pan of salted water to the boil. Add the
pasta, stir once and boil for 5 minutes. Add the
spinach, and cook for a further 3-5 minutes, until
tender. Drain well.

2 Melt the butter in a large pan and fry the bacon
for 5 minutes, until lightly browned. Stir in the
flour and cook for 1 minute. Gradually stir in the
milk, cooking until thickened and smooth. Simmer
for 1 minute.

3 Remove from heat and stir in the egg yolks,
nutmeg, pasta and spinach, Cheddar, half the
Parmesan and seasoning. Whisk egg whites until stiff
and fold in.

4 Turn into a buttered 1.8 litre (3 pint) soufflé dish
and sprinkle with remaining cheese. Bake for
25-30 minutes until well risen and golden brown.
Serve immediately.

MACARONI & VEGETABLE CHEESE

SERVES 4-6

Use whatever vegetables you have to hand. An ideal
recipe for using up small quantities.

250 g (8 oz) macaroni
250 g (8 oz) carrots, sliced
125 g (4 oz) French beans, cut into pieces
250 g (8 oz) cauliflower florets
1 leek, sliced
300 ml (½ pint) milk
40 g (1½ oz) butter
40 g (1½ oz) plain flour
2 teaspoons coarse-grain mustard
salt and pepper to taste
125 g (4 oz) mature Cheddar cheese, grated

1 Preheat the oven to 200°C (400°F/Gas 6). Bring a
large saucepan of salted water to the boil. Add
the macaroni, stir once and boil for 10-12 minutes
until tender.

2 Meanwhile cook the vegetables in salted water to
cover for 8-10 minutes, until just tender. Drain,
reserving 300 ml (½ pint) cooking liquid. Drain the
macaroni thoroughly and mix with the vegetables in a
buttered ovenproof dish.

3 Warm the milk. Melt the butter in a pan, add the
flour and cook for 1 minute. Add the milk and
vegetable stock and whisk over a moderate heat until
thickened and smooth. Add the mustard and
seasoning. Simmer for 1 minute. Remove from heat
and stir in half of the cheese.

4 Pour the sauce over the pasta and sprinkle with
remaining cheese. Bake for 15-20 minutes, until
golden brown and bubbling.

PASTA WITH
FISH & SHELLFISH

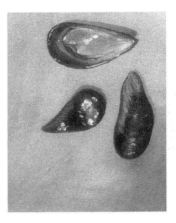

Pasta dishes featuring fish and shellfish can add a surprising dimension to your cooking. They tend to be light, yet satisfying, and can often turn a simple mean into something rather special. Try orecchiette with smoked trout and grainy mustard, or pappardelle with salmon and broccoli for a real treat. Canned fish – such as tuna, anchovies and baby clams – make great standbys for meals such as spaghetti with clams, or tuna and anchovy. Keep a pack of prawns in the freezer to make tasty pasta sauces, or an unusual stuffing for cannelloni.

CONTENTS

SPAGHETTI WITH TUNA & ANCHOVY

SERVES 4

This tuna and anchovy sauce – bursting with flavour – is just the thing to rustle up in a few minutes when you're in a hurry.

250g (8 oz) spaghetti
3 tablespoons olive oil
2 cloves garlic, chopped
½ chilli, seeded and chopped
25 g (1 oz) parsley, finely chopped
4 anchovy fillets, chopped
192 g (7 oz) can tuna in oil
salt and pepper to taste
parsley sprigs to garnish

1 Bring a large pan of salted water to the boil. Add the pasta, stir once and boil for 10-12 minutes until tender.

2 Meanwhile make the sauce. Heat the oil in a frying pan, add the garlic, chilli and parsley and fry gently, stirring, for 2 minutes. Add the anchovies and stir well until they start to dissolve.

3 Flake the tuna with its oil and add to the pan, stirring well. Season with pepper, and salt if necessary. Drain the pasta and mix together with the sauce. Serve immediately, garnished with parsley.

SPAGHETTI WITH CLAMS & LEEKS

SERVES 4

Keep a can of clams in your cupboard and you can put together this sauce in no time. When time is less pressing, use freshly cooked, shelled clams or mussels.

250 g (8 oz) spaghetti
25 g (1 oz) butter
2 leeks, thinly sliced
150 ml (¼ pint) dry white wine
pinch of powdered saffron
250 g (8 oz) can clams, drained
1 tablespoon chopped parsley
3 tablespoons double cream
salt and pepper to taste
parsley sprigs to garnish

1 Bring a large pan of salted water to the boil. Add the pasta, stir once and boil for 10-12 minutes until tender.

2 Meanwhile make the sauce. Melt the butter in a small pan, add the leeks and fry gently for about 5 minutes, until softened. Add the wine and saffron, bring to the boil, then boil steadily for about 5 minutes, until reduced by half.

3 Stir in the clams, parsley, cream, salt and pepper, then heat through gently.

4 Drain the spaghetti and toss with the sauce. Serve garnished with parsley.

FUSILLI WITH PRAWNS & BABY CORN

SERVES 4

Warm spices lend a subtle flavour to this delicious fish sauce.

250 g (8 oz) fusilli or pasta twists
125 g (4 oz) baby corn
75 g (3 oz) unsalted butter
250 g (8 oz) peeled prawns
¼ teaspoon ground mace
¼ teaspoon grated nutmeg
pinch of cayenne pepper
salt and pepper to taste
2 tablespoons chopped parsley

 Bring a large pan of salted water to the boil. Add the pasta, stir once and boil for 10-12 minutes until tender.

2 Meanwhile make the sauce. Cut the corn into thin diagonal slices. Melt the butter in a saucepan, add the corn and prawns and fry gently for 2-3 minutes. Sprinkle in the spices and stir well. Cover and cook gently for 2-3 minutes. Taste and add pepper, and salt if necessary.

3 Drain the pasta, pour over the sauce and toss well. Serve sprinkled with the parsley.

TAGLIATELLE WITH SMOKED SALMON & CUCUMBER

SERVES 4

The pink and green colours in this sauce look particularly good with a mixture of green and white tagliatelle.

250-350 g (8-12 oz) tagliatelle
50 g (2 oz) butter
½ teaspoon grated lemon rind
1 tablespoon chopped dill
½ cucumber, peeled and cut into sticks
150 ml (¼ pint) single cream
1 tablespoon lemon juice
125 g (4 oz) smoked salmon, cut into strips
dill sprigs to garnish

1 Bring a large pan of salted water to the boil. Add the pasta, stir once and boil for 8-10 minutes until tender.

2 Meanwhile make the sauce. Melt the butter in a saucepan, add the lemon rind and dill and stir well. Add the cucumber and cook gently for 5 minutes, stirring occasionally. Add the cream, lemon juice, salt and pepper and simmer for 2-3 minutes.

3 Gently stir in the salmon and heat through for 1-2 minutes.

4 Drain the pasta and mix with the sauce. Serve garnished with dill.

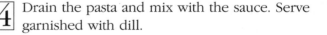

ORECCHIETTE WITH SMOKED TROUT

SERVES 4

For this recipe buy pieces of smoked trout fillet from the chilled counter, not the smoked trout which is prepared and packed like smoked salmon.

250 g (8 oz) orecchiette
½ bunch watercress
125 g (4 oz) smoked trout fillet
125 g (4 oz) curd cheese
2 teaspoons coarse-grain mustard
2 tablespoons dry white wine
150 ml (¼ pint) single cream
salt and pepper to taste
freshly shredded Parmesan cheese to serve

1 Bring a large pan of salted water to the boil. Add the pasta, stir once and boil for 10-12 minutes until tender.

2 Meanwhile make the sauce. Chop the watercress roughly. Cut the trout into small strips. Place the curd cheese, mustard, wine and cream in a small saucepan and heat gently, stirring, until thickened and smooth. Add the watercress, trout, salt and pepper; heat through gently for 2-3 minutes.

3 Drain the pasta and mix with the sauce, tossing thoroughly. Serve sprinkled with shreds of Parmesan cheese.

RIGATONI WITH BROCCOLI & ANCHOVIES

SERVES 4

I have based this recipe on one from Sicily, where broccoli and anchovy are a popular combination.

250-350 g (8-12 oz) rigatoni
4 tablespoons olive oil
2 cloves garlic, chopped
25 g (1 oz) pine nuts
50 g (1¾ oz) can anchovies
350 g (12 oz) broccoli, cut into small florets
¼ teaspoon chilli powder

1 Bring a large pan of salted water to the boil. Add the pasta, stir once and boil for 10-12 minutes until tender. Drain well.

2 Meanwhile, make the sauce. Heat the oil in a frying pan, add the garlic and pine nuts and fry for a few minutes, until the nuts are lightly browned. Chop the anchovies and add to the pan, together with their oil. Heat gently, mashing the anchovies into the oil until they start to dissolve.

3 Add the broccoli and stir well. Cover and cook gently for 5 minutes, until just tender. Add the chilli powder, taste and add salt if necessary.

4 Mix the sauce with the drained pasta and serve.

PRAWN & RED PEPPER CANNELLONI

SERVES 4

I find it easier to roll up sheets of lasagne, than trying to stuff cannelloni tubes.

250 g (8 oz) can red peppers, drained and finely chopped
125 g (4 oz) peeled prawns, chopped
125 g (4 oz) ricotta cheese
2 tablespoons fromage frais
2 teaspoons paprika
¼ teaspoon chilli powder
salt and pepper to taste
175 g (6 oz) fresh lasagne
450 ml (¾ pint) milk
25 g (1 oz) butter
25 g (1 oz) plain flour
50 g (2 oz) grated gruyère cheese
1 tablespoon dried wholemeal breadcrumbs
parsley sprigs to garnish

1 Preheat oven to 180°C (350°F/Gas 4). In a bowl, mix together the chopped peppers, prawns, ricotta, fromage frais, paprika, chilli and salt. Lay the lasagne sheets on a work surface. Spread a little filling along one long side of each sheet and roll up loosely, enclosing the filling. Place close together in a shallow ovenproof dish.

2 Warm the milk. Melt the butter in a small pan, stir in the flour and cook for 1 minute. Whisk in the milk, then cook, stirring, until thickened and smooth. Season.

3 Pour the sauce over the pasta and sprinkle with gruyère and breadcrumbs. Bake for 25 minutes, or until the pasta is cooked and the topping is golden brown. Garnish with parsley to serve.

BAKED HADDOCK PASTA

SERVES 4

Make this complete meal for all the family – the children will love it!

250 g (8 oz) pasta knots or twists
600 ml (1 pint) milk
40 g (1½ oz) butter
40 g (1½ oz) plain flour
freshly grated nutmeg to taste
salt and pepper to taste
500 g (1 lb) skinned smoked haddock, cubed
3 tomatoes, skinned and quartered
4 spring onions, chopped
1 tablespoon dried white breadcrumbs
50 g (2 oz) double Gloucester cheese, grated

1 Preheat oven to 180°C (350°F/Gas 4). Bring a large pan of salted water to the boil. Add the pasta, stir once and boil for 10-12 minutes until tender.

2 Meanwhile make the sauce. Warm the milk. Melt the butter in a small saucepan, stir in the flour and cook for 1 minute. Whisk in the milk and cook, stirring, until the sauce is thickened and smooth. Season with nutmeg, salt and pepper.

3 Drain the pasta and toss in a little oil to prevent sticking. Lightly mix with the haddock, tomatoes, spring onions and sauce.

4 Turn into a buttered ovenproof dish and sprinkle with the breadcrumbs and cheese. Bake for 30 minutes, until the topping is golden brown.

ABOVE: PRAWN & RED PEPPER CANNELLONI *BELOW*: BAKED HADDOCK PASTA

PAPPARDELLE WITH SALMON & BROCCOLI

SERVES 4

250 g (8 oz) pappardelle
250 g (8 oz) broccoli florets
25 g (1 oz) butter
1 tablespoon sunflower oil
1 small leek, sliced
1 teaspoon chopped fresh root ginger
250 g (8 oz) skinned salmon fillet, cubed
150 ml (¼ pint) dry white wine
salt and pepper to taste
3 tablespoons fromage frais
snipped chives to garnish

1 Bring a large pan of salted water to the boil. Add the pasta, stir once and boil for 10-12 minutes until tender.

2 Meanwhile make the sauce. Parcook the broccoli in boiling salted water for 2 minutes; drain. Heat the butter and oil in a saucepan, add the leek and ginger and fry, stirring, for 1 minute. Add the broccoli and salmon and stir around gently. Add the wine and seasoning. Bring to the boil, then cover and simmer for 2-3 minutes, until the salmon is tender.

3 Lower the heat and stir in the fromage frais, a spoonful at a time. Taste and adjust seasoning if necessary.

4 Drain the pasta and mix with the sauce. Serve sprinkled with chives.

PASTA WITH SPICED PRAWNS & CAULIFLOWER

SERVES 4

A deliciously different winter dish.

250 g (8 oz) pasta twists
5 tablespoons sunflower oil
2 cloves garlic, chopped
1 teaspoon cumin seeds
1 teaspoon mustard seeds
250 g (8 oz) cauliflower florets
½ red pepper, seeded and finely chopped
250 g (8 oz) peeled prawns
1 teaspoon paprika
salt to taste
1 teaspoon sesame oil

1 Bring a large pan of salted water to the boil. Add the pasta, stir once and boil for 10-12 minutes until tender. Drain well.

2 Meanwhile, heat the oil in a large frying pan or wok. Add the garlic, cumin and mustard seeds and stir-fry for 1 minute. Add the cauliflower and stir-fry for a further 1-2 minutes until the cauliflower begins to colour. Lower the heat, cover and cook for 5 minutes, stirring occasionally.

3 Add the red pepper, prawns, paprika and salt. Stir well, then cook, covered, for a further 2-3 minutes.

4 Just before serving, add the drained pasta, drizzle in the sesame oil and toss together.

ABOVE: PAPPARDELLE WITH SALMON & BROCCOLI *BELOW*: PASTA WITH SPICED PRAWNS & CAULIFLOWER

STIR-FRIED THAI NOODLES

SERVES 4

250 g (8 oz) flat rice noodles
4 tablespoons sunflower oil
2 rashers smoked streaky bacon, diced
1 clove garlic, crushed
1 red chilli, seeded and chopped
250 g (8 oz) peeled prawns
125 g (8 oz) mooli, peeled and chopped
25 g (1 oz) creamed coconut
150 ml (¼ pint) boiling water
2 teaspoons soft brown sugar
2 tablespoons lime juice
1 tablespoon crunchy peanut butter
125 g (4 oz) beansprouts
salt to taste
6 spring onions, shredded

1 Soak the noodles in hot water for 15 minutes until soft; drain thoroughly.

2 Heat the oil in a large frying pan or wok, add the bacon and fry until crispy. Add the garlic, chilli, prawns and mooli and mix well.

3 Blend the creamed coconut with the water, then add the sugar, lime juice and peanut butter. Add to the mixture in the frying pan, stir well and simmer for 2 minutes.

4 Add the noodles, beansprouts, salt and half of the spring onions. Stir, then cook gently for 3-4 minutes, stirring occasionally.

5 Serve sprinkled with the remaining spring onions.

TAGLIATELLE WITH PRAWNS & MUSHROOMS

SERVES 4

Tiger prawns have distinctive dark pink stripes. They are now fairly easy to buy from supermarkets and fish counters. Use a mixture of green and white tagliatelle. Illustrated on back cover.

250-350 g (8-12 oz) tagliatelle
25 g (1 oz) butter
125 g (4 oz) button mushrooms, sliced
250 g (8 oz) tiger prawns
75 g (3 oz) curd cheese
2 tablespoons snipped chives
150 ml (¼ pint) single cream
salt and pepper to taste
25 g (1 oz) pine nuts, toasted
freshly grated Parmesan cheese to serve

1 Bring a large pan of salted water to the boil. Add the pasta, stir once and boil for 8-10 minutes until tender.

2 Meanwhile make the sauce. Heat the butter in a frying pan, add the mushrooms and fry for 2-3 minutes. Add the prawns and stir well. Add the curd cheese and stir around until it begins to melt. Add the chives, cream, salt and pepper and bring to a gentle simmer.

3 Drain the pasta and mix with the sauce. Serve sprinkled with pine nuts and accompanied by freshly grated Parmesan.

PASTA WITH MEAT

Less is more is the motto for this chapter! A little meat goes a long way in pasta dishes, where the meat is used mainly to add flavour and enrich the sauce. The balance of plenty of vegetables and pasta to a little meat is a healthy one, particularly favoured by the Chinese and I have followed their example in the stir-fries in this chapter. Baked pasta with a thin layer of meat sauce provides a heart-warming meal. Flavour-packed cured meats – such as chorizo sausage, bacon and prosciutto – make delicious bases for simple sauces.

CONTENTS

PENNE WITH CHORIZO & CORN

SERVES 4

I used hot chorizo sausage for this sauce; it gives a deliciously fiery taste. If you prefer a milder flavour, use sweet chorizo which is lightly spiced with paprika.

250 g (8 oz) penne
1 tablespoon olive oil
1 small onion, thinly sliced
350 g (12 oz) chorizo sausage, sliced
125 g (4 oz) baby corn
salt to taste
1 tablespoon chopped parsley

1 Bring a large saucepan of salted water to the boil. Add the penne, stir once and boil for 10-12 minutes until tender. Drain well.

2 Meanwhile make the sauce. Heat the oil in a frying pan, add the onion and fry for about 5 minutes, until lightly browned. Add the sausage and fry, stirring, for 5 minutes until turning crisp. Add the baby corn and cook for 2 minutes. Taste and add salt if necessary.

3 Mix the penne and sauce. Serve immediately, sprinkled with parsley.

TORTELLONI WITH SALAMI & SUN-DRIED TOMATOES

SERVES 4

Served with this flavoursome sauce, spinach and ricotta tortelloni provides a substantial meal. For a lighter meal or a tasty starter, serve the sauce with fine tagliatelle instead.

50 g (2 oz) sun-dried tomatoes in oil
1 tablespoon oil (from tomato jar)
2 tablespoons olive oil
2 cloves garlic, finely chopped
50 g (2 oz) Italian salami, chopped
1 teaspoon Dijon mustard
2 tablespoons chopped parsley
1 tablespoon lemon juice
350 g (12 oz) spinach & ricotta tortelloni
parsley sprigs to garnish

1 Chop the sun-dried tomatoes into small pieces, then place in a saucepan with the oils, garlic, salami, mustard, parsley and lemon juice. Mix well and leave to marinade for a few minutes.

2 Bring a large saucepan of salted water to the boil. Add the tortelloni, stir once and boil for 12-15 minutes until tender. Halfway through the cooking time, warm the sauce through gently.

3 Drain the pasta and return it to the pan. Add the sauce, toss well and serve immediately, garnished with parsley.

CHICKEN & VEGETABLE CANNELLONI

SERVES 4

Fresh lasagne is quick-cooking and easy to use. Here it encloses a light fresh-tasting chicken filling. A great supper dish, perfect served with a simple crisp salad.

350 g (12 oz) boneless chicken breasts
2 carrots, finely chopped
2 sticks celery, finely chopped
2 shallots, finely chopped
bouquet garni
150 ml (¼ pint) vegetable stock
150 ml (¼ pint) white wine
salt and pepper to taste
125 g (4 oz) curd cheese
2 teaspoons chopped marjoram
1 tablespoon lemon juice
300 g (10 oz) fresh lasagne
300 ml (½ pint) milk (approximately)
25 g (1 oz) butter
25 g (1 oz) plain flour
2 tablespoons freshly grated Parmesan cheese

1 Preheat oven to 190°C (375°F/Gas 5). Cut the chicken into 2.5 cm (1 inch) chunks and place in a saucepan with the carrots, celery, shallots and bouquet garni. Add the stock, wine, salt and pepper. Bring to the boil, cover and simmer for 15 minutes, or until the chicken is tender.

2 Strain the chicken and vegetables, reserving the stock. Discard the bouquet garni.

3 Place the chicken and vegetables in a food processor with 2 tablespoons of the stock. Process until the chicken is finely chopped, then add the curd cheese, marjoram and lemon juice. Process for a few seconds until evenly mixed. Taste and adjust seasoning if necessary.

4 Cut each sheet of lasagne in half, spread with a little of the chicken filling and roll up.

5 Make the stock up to 450 ml (¾ pint) with milk and heat gently. Melt the butter in a saucepan, add the flour and cook for 1 minute. Add the warmed liquid and bring to the boil, whisking all the time, until the sauce is thickened and smooth. Season with salt and pepper.

6 Spread a thin layer of sauce over the base of a buttered shallow oblong ovenproof dish. Arrange the pasta rolls on top, a little apart, then pour over the remaining sauce. Sprinkle with Parmesan and bake in the oven for 25-30 minutes until golden brown. Serve with a salad.

PASTA WITH COURGETTES & 'BACON'

SERVES 4

A great dish if you are in a hurry, as it uses few ingredients and is cooked in minutes. Pancetta – Italian cured pork – is ideal for this. It is similar in taste to a mild cured bacon, which is a good substitute.

250 g (8 oz) ondule or pasta shells
3 tablespoons olive oil
125 g (4 oz) pancetta or mild streaky bacon,
  chopped
175 g (6 oz) courgettes, shredded
1-2 tablespoons lemon juice
salt and pepper to taste
good handful of basil leaves

1 Bring a large saucepan of salted water to the boil. Coil in the ondule or add the pasta shells and boil for 10-12 minutes until tender.

2 Meanwhile, heat 1 tablespoon oil in a large saucepan, add the pancetta or bacon and fry for 5 minutes, or until slightly crisp. Add the remaining oil and when hot, add the courgettes and stir well. Lower the heat, cover and cook for 2 minutes.

3 Stir in the lemon juice, pepper and half of the basil leaves, torn if large. Simmer for 2 minutes. Taste and add salt if necessary.

4 Drain the cooked pasta thoroughly and add to the sauce ingredients. Stir well and serve immediately, garnished with the remaining basil.

TAGLIATELLE WITH PROSCIUTTO & VEGETABLE RIBBONS

SERVES 4

For an economical alternative, use cooked ham instead of prosciutto.

125 g (4 oz) prosciutto
2 carrots
2-3 courgettes
250-350 g (8-12 oz) fresh or dried tagliatelle
50 g (2 oz) butter
50 g (2 oz) freshly grated Parmesan cheese
pepper to taste

1 Cut the prosciutto into thin strips. Using a potato peeler, pare the carrots and courgettes lengthwise into ribbons.

2 Bring a large saucepan of salted water to the boil. Add the pasta, stir once and boil for 4-5 minutes for fresh pasta; 8-10 minutes for dried.

3 Meanwhile make the sauce. Melt the butter in a frying pan, add the prosciutto and stir-fry for 1 minute. Add the vegetable ribbons and stir-fry for 2-3 minutes.

4 Drain the pasta and place in a large warmed dish. Add the vegetable mixture, Parmesan and plenty of pepper. Stir well, tossing all the ingredients together. Serve immediately.

ABOVE: PASTA WITH COURGETTES & 'BACON' *BELOW*: TAGLIATELLE WITH PROSCIUTTO & VEGETABLE RIBBONS

STIR-FRIED BEEF WITH NOODLES

SERVES 4

Once you have all the ingredients assembled and prepared, this dish takes only a few minutes to cook. It works equally well with chicken and pork. To make it easier to cut the meat into wafer-thin slices, wrap it in freezer wrap and freeze for 30 minutes before slicing.

---

250 g (8 oz) broccoli
350 g (12 oz) skirt of beef
2 tablespoons dry sherry
2 tablespoons soy sauce
2 teaspoons cornflour
250 g (8 oz) Chinese egg noodles
4 tablespoons sunflower oil
1 clove garlic, crushed
1 teaspoon grated fresh root ginger
1 onion, thinly sliced
125 g (4 oz) mushrooms, thinly sliced
300 ml (½ pint) boiling water
125 g (4 oz) beansprouts
2 spring onions, sliced diagonally

1 Break up the broccoli florets into small pieces, then slice the stalks thinly on the diagonal.

2 Slice the beef as thinly as possible across the grain, then place in a bowl with the sherry, soy sauce and cornflour. Stir well to coat evenly.

3 Bring a large saucepan of salted water to the boil. Add the noodles, remove from the heat, cover and leave for 6 minutes. Drain well and toss in a little oil.

4 Meanwhile, heat half the oil in a large frying pan or wok. Add the garlic and ginger and stir-fry for 1 minute. Add the onion and stir-fry for 1 minute. Add the broccoli and mushrooms and stir-fry for 1 minute. Remove all the vegetables from the pan with a slotted spoon and transfer to a plate.

5 Add the remaining oil to the pan. When it is hot, add the meat and stir-fry quickly until browned, about 2 minutes. Add the boiling water and bring to the boil, stirring. Return the vegetables to the pan, stir well and cook for 1 minute.

6 Add the beansprouts and noodles, bring to the boil, then cover and cook for 2 minutes.

7 Serve immediately, sprinkled with the spring onions.

GNOCCHI WITH SAGE & PROSCIUTTO

SERVES 4

500 g (1 lb) medium-sized floury potatoes
salt and pepper to taste
150 g (5 oz) plain flour
1 egg, beaten

SAUCE
8-10 sage leaves, chopped
150 ml (¼ pint) single cream
125 g (4 oz) frozen broad beans, cooked
25 g (1 oz) prosciutto, thinly sliced

TO SERVE
freshly grated Parmesan cheese

1 Cook the potatoes in their skins in boiling salted water until tender, about 20-25 minutes; drain. When cool enough to handle, peel off the skins and mash the potatoes. Add salt, pepper, flour and egg; mix well.

2 Divide the dough in half and form each into a long sausage shape on a lightly floured surface. Cut into 2.5 cm (1 inch) lengths and mark each by rolling along the prongs of a fork.

3 Place all the ingredients for the sauce in a small pan and simmer gently for a few minutes.

4 Bring a large pan of salted water to the boil. Add the gnocchi and simmer for 4-5 minutes, until they float to the surface. Remove with a slotted spoon and divide between warmed dishes. Pour over the sauce and serve with Parmesan.

PASTA WITH CHICKEN LIVER & SAGE SAUCE

SERVES 4

500 g (1 lb) chicken livers, defrosted if frozen
4 tablespoons olive oil
3 shallots, chopped
1 tablespoon chopped sage leaves
2 tablespoons tomato purée
150 ml (¼ pint) beef consommé
150 ml (¼ pint) water
salt and pepper to taste
2 tablespoons brandy
250-350 g (8-12 oz) pasta shells
1 tablespoon dried breadcrumbs
2 tablespoons chopped parsley

1 Rinse and dry the chicken livers, then cut into small pieces. Heat half of the oil in a saucepan, add the shallots and fry gently for 3-4 minutes. Add the sage and chicken livers and cook over a high heat, stirring until the livers are evenly browned.

2 Add the tomato purée, consommé, water, salt, pepper and brandy. Bring to the boil, cover and simmer for 12-15 minutes.

3 Meanwhile bring a large saucepan of salted water to the boil. Add the pasta, stir once and boil for 10-12 minutes until tender; drain.

4 Heat the remaining oil in the pan, add the breadcrumbs and half of the parsley and fry for 1-2 minutes, until crisp. Add the pasta and toss well.

5 Serve the pasta topped with the sauce and sprinkled with the remaining parsley.

ABOVE: GNOCCHI WITH SAGE & PROSCIUTTO *BELOW*: PASTA WITH CHICKEN LIVER & SAGE SAUCE

PASTA SPIRALS WITH PORK MEATBALLS

SERVES 4

Make these tasty meatballs in quantity for feeding a crowd, or freeze some for unexpected guests.

MEATBALLS
500 g (1 lb) minced pork
grated rind of ½ lemon
25 g (1 oz) wholemeal breadcrumbs
1 teaspoon soy sauce
1 egg, beaten
salt and pepper to taste
2 tablespoons olive oil

SAUCE
2 cloves garlic, peeled
1 onion, roughly chopped
2 carrots, roughly chopped
2 sticks celery, roughly chopped
1 red pepper, cored, seeded and roughly chopped
2 teaspoons dried oregano
397 g (14 oz) can chopped tomatoes
150 ml (¼ pint) vegetable stock
1 tablespoon lemon juice
250-350 g (8-12 oz) pasta spirals
1 tablespoon chopped parsley

TO GARNISH
parsley sprigs

1 To prepare the meatballs, put the pork, lemon rind, breadcrumbs, soy sauce, egg, salt and pepper into a bowl and mix together, using your hands, until evenly blended. Shape the mixture into about 30 small balls.

2 Heat 1 tablespoon of the oil in a saucepan, add the meatballs and fry for about 5 minutes until lightly browned. Remove from the pan using a slotted spoon and transfer to a plate. Drain off all but 1 tablespoon of the oil from the pan.

3 To make the sauce, place the garlic, onion, carrots, celery and red pepper in a food processor or blender and work until finely chopped. Add to the pan and cook, stirring, for 2-3 minutes. Add the oregano, chopped tomatoes, stock, lemon juice, salt and pepper and bring to the boil.

4 Return the meatballs to the pan and simmer, covered, for 15 minutes.

5 Meanwhile cook the pasta. Bring a large saucepan of salted water to the boil. Add the pasta spirals, stir once and boil for 10-12 minutes until tender. Drain well and return to the pan. Add the parsley and remaining 1 tablespoon oil; toss well.

6 Serve the pasta topped with the meatballs in sauce, and garnished with parsley.

CREAMY BOWS WITH BACON & MUSHROOMS

SERVES 4

This dish is always a winner. It is also made with ingredients you are likely to have to hand. In place of the soft cheese I suggest, you can use curd cheese and flavour it with some parsley and garlic.

250-350 g (8-12 oz) pasta bows
1 tablespoon olive oil
4 rashers streaky bacon, derinded and chopped
125 g (4 oz) button mushrooms, sliced
75 g (3 oz) soft cheese with garlic & herbs
150 ml (¼ pint) single cream
salt and pepper to taste
chopped parsley to garnish
freshly grated cheese Parmesan to serve

1 Bring a large saucepan of salted water to the boil. Add the pasta, stir once and boil for 10-12 minutes until tender.

2 Meanwhile make the sauce. Heat the oil in a frying pan, add the bacon and fry until lightly browned and crisp, about 5 minutes. Add the mushrooms and cook for 2-3 minutes, until softened.

3 Lower the heat and add the soft cheese, mashing it down until it begins to melt. Pour in the cream and heat gently, stirring to form a thick sauce. Add seasoning.

4 Drain the pasta, return to the pan and add the sauce. Toss well and serve, sprinkled with chopped parsley and Parmesan.

FETTUCINE WITH SMOKED HAM & ARTICHOKES

SERVES 4

This sauce tastes very good with fresh herb and garlic flavoured pasta, or three coloured pasta. If you are using fresh pasta, reduce the cooking time to 3-4 minutes.

250 g (8 oz) fettucine
400 g (14 oz) can artichoke hearts
400 g (14 oz) thick slice oak smoked ham
3 tablespoons olive oil
1 clove garlic, chopped
2 tablespoons chopped mint
1 tablespoon lemon juice
salt and pepper to taste
3 tablespoons single cream
parsley sprigs to garnish

1 Bring a large pan of salted water to the boil. Add the fettucine, stir once and boil for 8-10 minutes until tender. Drain well.

2 Meanwhile make the sauce. Drain the artichokes and rinse under cold running water; drain well and pat dry with kitchen paper. Slice the artichokes. Dice the ham.

3 Heat the oil in a saucepan, add the artichokes and fry gently for 2 minutes, stirring carefully. Add the garlic, ham and mint and fry, stirring, for 2 minutes. Add the lemon juice and pepper and heat through. Taste and add salt if necessary. Stir in the cream and warm through gently.

4 Toss the pasta with the sauce. Serve immediately, garnished with parsley.

ABOVE: CREAMY BOWS WITH BACON & MUSHROOMS *BELOW:* FETTUCINE WITH SMOKED HAM & ARTICHOKES

BAKED MACARONI WITH MEAT SAUCE

SERVES 4

This dish can be completely assembled several hours before you wish to serve it, in which case the baking time must be increased to 25 minutes.

1 tablespoon olive oil
1 clove garlic, crushed
4 rashers smoked streaky bacon, derinded and
    chopped
1 small onion, chopped
250 g (8 oz) lean minced lamb
salt and pepper to taste
½ teaspoon dried marjoram
2 tablespoons chopped parsley
125 ml (4 fl oz) dry white wine
250 g (8 oz) passata
250 g (8 oz) macaroni

SAUCE
300 ml (½ pint) milk
25 g (1 oz) butter
25 g (1 oz) plain flour
freshly grated nutmeg to taste

TO FINISH
125 g (4 oz) gruyère cheese, grated
thyme sprigs to garnish

1 Preheat oven to 200°C (400°F/Gas 6). Heat the oil in a saucepan. Add the garlic, bacon and onion and fry for about 5 minutes, until the onion is lightly browned. Add the lamb and fry, stirring, until evenly coloured. Add the salt, pepper, herbs, wine and passata and bring to the boil. Simmer, uncovered, for about 20 minutes, stirring occasionally.

2 Meanwhile, bring a large saucepan of salted water to the boil. Add the macaroni, stir once and boil for 10-12 minutes until tender.

3 To make the sauce, heat the milk. Melt the butter in a small saucepan, stir in the flour and cook for 1 minute. Add the milk all at once and bring to the boil, whisking all the time, until the sauce is thickened and smooth. Season with salt, pepper and nutmeg.

4 Drain the macaroni and spread half of it in a buttered ovenproof dish. Pour over half of the meat sauce. Cover with the remaining macaroni, then the rest of the meat sauce. Top with the white sauce and sprinkle with cheese.

5 Bake in the oven for 15 minutes, until bubbling and golden brown. If the top is not sufficiently browned, place under a preheated hot grill for 2-3minutes. Garnish with thyme to serve.

GREEK LAMB WITH ORZO

SERVES 4-5

Orzo – also called puntalette – is tiny pasta shaped like rice grains. It soaks up all the delicious cooking juices. Although the cooking time is long, it is assembled in minutes and needs little attention.

750 g (1½ lb) boneless lamb
2 onions, sliced
2 tablespoons lemon juice
salt and pepper to taste
1 tablespoon chopped oregano
1 teaspoon ground cumin
½ teaspoon ground cinnamon
1 tablespoon olive oil
2 tablespoons tomato purée
900 ml (1½ pints) boiling water
250 g (8 oz) orzo

TO SERVE
oregano leaves to garnish
freshly shredded Parmesan cheese

1 Preheat oven to 180°C (350°F/Gas 4). Cut the lamb into 4 cm (1½ inch) cubes and place in a large casserole dish. Add the onions, lemon juice, seasoning, oregano, cumin and cinnamon. Mix well, then drizzle over the oil. Bake, uncovered, for 1 hour.

2 Mix together the tomato purée and boiling water and pour over the lamb. Cover and cook in the oven for 30 minutes.

3 Add the orzo, stir well, then cover and return to the oven for 30 minutes. Serve sprinkled with oregano leaves and Parmesan.

PENNE WITH RICH SAUSAGE SAUCE

SERVES 4-6

Choose good quality Italian or Cumberland sausages for this dish.

500 g (1 lb) sausages, skins removed
2 tablespoons olive oil
1 onion, thinly sliced
150 ml (¼ pint) red wine
397 g (14 oz) can chopped tomatoes
1 tablespoon tomato purée
125 g (4 oz) mushrooms, sliced
salt and pepper to taste
250-350 g (8-12 oz) penne
25 g (1 oz) butter
2 tablespoons freshly grated Parmesan cheese
herb sprigs to garnish

1 Shape each sausage into 4-5 small balls. Heat the oil in a deep frying pan, add the meatballs and fry until evenly browned, about 5 minutes. Spoon off any excess oil, leaving a little in the pan, then add the onion and fry for 5 minutes.

2 Add the wine, tomatoes, tomato purée, mushrooms, salt and pepper. Bring to the boil, stirring gently. Lower the heat, cover and simmer for 15-20 minutes.

3 Meanwhile bring a large pan of salted water to the boil. Add the pasta, stir once and boil for 10-12 minutes until tender.

4 Drain the pasta thoroughly, then return to the pan, add the butter and Parmesan and stir over a low heat until the butter has melted. Serve piping hot, topped with the sausage sauce and herbs.

ABOVE: GREEK LAMB WITH ORZO *BELOW:* PENNE WITH RICH SAUSAGE SAUCE

CHICKEN RICE NOODLES

SERVES 4

250 g (8 oz) chicken thighs
3 slices fresh root ginger
4 cloves garlic
5 spring onions, chopped
1.2 litres (2 pints) water
1 teaspoon salt
250 g (8 oz) rice noodles
2 tablespoons soy sauce
2 tablespoons dry sherry
175 g (6 oz) carrots, thinly sliced
125 g (4 oz) shitake mushrooms, sliced
250 g (8 oz) spinach leaves, shredded
pepper to taste

1 Place the chicken in a large pan with the ginger, garlic, half the spring onions, the water and salt. Bring slowly to the boil, skim, then partly cover and simmer for 20 minutes.

2 Meanwhile, put the rice noodles in a bowl and pour on boiling water to cover. Leave to soak for 15 minutes until softened.

3 Strain the chicken stock and return to the pan. Add the soy sauce and sherry and bring to a simmer. Skin the chicken and strip the meat from the bones. Cut the meat into thin strips and add to the stock with the carrots. Simmer for 5 minutes.

4 Drain the noodles and add to the pan with the mushrooms, spinach and pepper. Simmer for 2 minutes. Serve in bowls, sprinkled with the reserved spring onions.

CHINESE NOODLES WITH PORK

SERVES 4

250 g (8 oz) pork fillet, finely sliced
2 tablespoons soy sauce
2 tablespoons cornflour
5 spring onions, shredded
250 g (8 oz) Chinese egg noodles
4 tablespoons sunflower oil
1 teaspoon chopped fresh root ginger
75 g (3 oz) baby corn, halved lengthwise
75 g (3 oz) mangetout, trimmed
175 g (6 oz) mushrooms, sliced
50 g (2 oz) canned bamboo shoots, sliced
1 tablespoon tomato purée
1 tablespoon dry sherry

1 Mix the pork with 1 tablespoon soy sauce, the cornflour and half the spring onions in a bowl.

2 Bring a large pan of salted water to the boil. Add the noodles, cover and leave to stand off the heat for 6 minutes. Drain well.

3 Heat 2 tablespoons oil in a large frying pan or wok. Add the pork and stir-fry for 1-2 minutes, until lightly browned; remove.

4 Add the remaining oil to the pan and, when hot, add the ginger, corn, mangetout, mushrooms and bamboo shoots. Stir-fry for 1 minute.

5 Blend the remaining soy sauce with the tomato purée, sherry and 5 tablespoons water. Add to the pan with the pork. Stir, then cover and cook for 3-4 minutes, until the pork is tender.

6 Add the noodles, toss well and heat through. Serve sprinkled with the remaining spring onions.

SPINACH & PROSCIUTTO ROLLS

SERVES 4

Thin strips of fresh lasagne are rolled up and baked Chelsea-bun-style to show off the colourful filling of spinach and prosciutto. Double or triple quantities for party cooking. Illustrated on back cover.

25 g (1 oz) butter
2 shallots, finely chopped
500 g (1 lb) frozen leaf spinach, defrosted
freshly grated nutmeg to taste
salt and pepper to taste
2 tablespoons double cream
8 sheets fresh lasagne
12 slices prosciutto
40 g (1½ oz) freshly grated Parmesan cheese

SAUCE
50 g (2 oz) butter
40 g (1½ oz) plain flour
600 ml (1 pint) milk

1 Preheat oven to 200°C (400°F/Gas 6). Melt the butter in a small pan, add the shallots and fry gently for 2-3 minutes, until softened. Transfer to a bowl.

2 Drain the spinach thoroughly in a sieve, pressing out as much liquid as possible, then chop finely. Add the spinach, nutmeg, salt, pepper and cream to the shallots and mix well.

3 Cut each sheet of lasagne lengthwise into 3 strips. Cut the slices of prosciutto in half lengthwise. Lay a slice of prosciutto on each strip of lasagne. Divide the spinach mixture between the strips and spread evenly over the prosciutto. Sprinkle with a little of the Parmesan, then roll up loosely.

4 Place the spinach and prosciutto rolls, cut sides up, close together in a buttered shallow ovenproof dish.

5 To make the sauce, melt the butter in a small pan. Stir in the flour and cook, stirring, for 1 minute. Gradually add the milk, stirring all the time, until the sauce is thickened and smooth. Simmer, stirring, for 1 minute, then season with salt, pepper and nutmeg.

6 Pour the sauce over the spinach and prosciutto rolls and sprinkle with the remaining Parmesan. Bake in the oven for 25 minutes, until the topping is golden brown. Serve with a crisp green salad.

INDEX

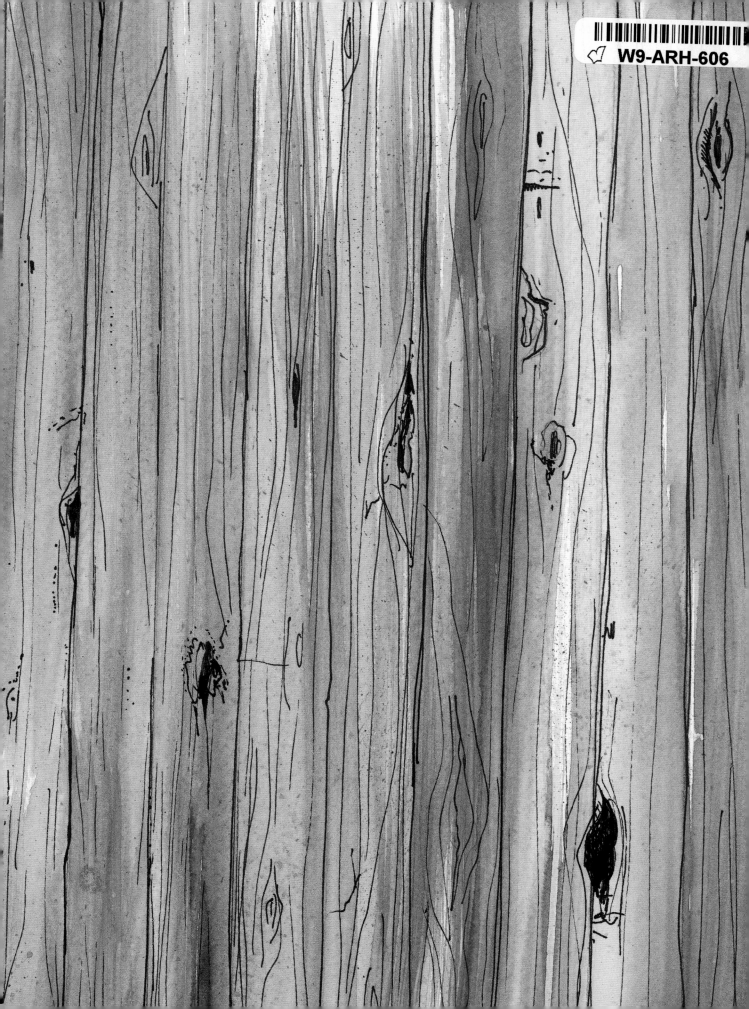

ISBN 978-0-9905603-1-9

Design:
David Robson, Robson Design

Published by
AMPERSAND, INC.
1050 North State Street
Chicago, Illinois 60610
—
203 Finland Place
New Orleans, Louisiana 70131

www.ampersandworks.com

Produced and Published in the United States
Printed in U.S.A.
10 8 6 4 2   3 5 7 9

The Mom's Choice Awards® Honoring Excellence
logo is a trademark of the Mom's Choice Awards.

To request a personalized copy or to schedule
a book signing/school reading, email
nancyegee@sbcglobal.net

www.anancygeebook.com

a nancy gee book

The
SECRET
DRAWER

Written by Nancy Gee • Illustrated by Raye Ann Saunoris

Enjoy all the surprises of nature!
Nancy Gee

AMP&RSAND, INC.
Chicago • New Orleans

In memory of my mother, who was an avid reader
and a woman who loved nature
and all animals.

"Maddie, I'm done painting, it's time to run.
I'm leaving now to have some fun.

"The door is open, so shut it tight.
The sun is setting. I'll say goodnight."

Two friends play under a moonlit sky
In the forest that's nearby.

"Al, can you see me in the trees,
Swinging with the greatest of ease?

"Trees, trees everywhere!
We can play without a care."

"Sal, can you see me down below,
Splashing water as it flows?

"Water, water everywhere.
We can play without a care!"

"Come on, Sal, and follow me.
There's so much more for us to see.

"Feeders, feeders everywhere!
A feeder here, a feeder there,
I see feeders everywhere!"

"Treats, treats everywhere.
We can eat without a care.
I see treats everywhere!"

The feeder swings from Al's big leap.
Raining food for them to eat.

The feeder tips from side-to-side.
Hold on! Oh, what a ride!

Noises, noises from out there.
Noises, noises everywhere.

A broken feeder hits the ground,
Making such a terrible sound!

"Kitty, you were keeping guard!
Who has done this to my yard?"

"Al, here she comes, we must scurry.
No time to waste, we must hurry.

"Back to the woods, back to the trees,
There we'll be safe, playing in the breeze."

"Run, Al, run! Run along the rail.
At its end we can sail!"

"Al, what are you doing?
Where did you go?
What are you thinking?
I just don't know.

"Into the house you must've gone.
Into a place you do not belong!"

Maddie exclaims, "Oh, my dear!
What in the world is going on out here?

"This door's not shut, not at all.
And my feeders have taken a fall.

"Kitty, Kitty we must close the door tight,
Put everything back until it's just right."

"Oh, no, Al! I am out and you are in.
The door is closed . . . you're stuck within.

"Poor Al, trapped inside this house,
You must be quick and quiet as a mouse.

"Kitty's inside now . . . sniffing about.
HIDE, AL, HIDE! You can't get out!"

"Look out Al, you must be brave.
Kitty's back, he won't behave.

"Low and slow I watch him creep
I'm sure he's ready to make his leap."

"I saw you jump up from the floor.
Right into that open drawer.

The leap you made was just in time.
That Kitty was right behind!"

"You are safe now in the drawer.
Kitty can't reach you anymore."

"Al, can you hear me from outside?
You have found a good place to hide.

"How are you doing? Are you scared?
The lady is coming . . . be prepared!"

"A sock drawer is no place to play.
Get off that dresser! Right away!"

"The drawer is shut. Now leap down.
Get down, Kitty! Don't make me frown!

"Come along, Kitty, let it be.
Come along, Kitty, follow me."

"Now there is no time to waste.
They are gone, we must make haste."

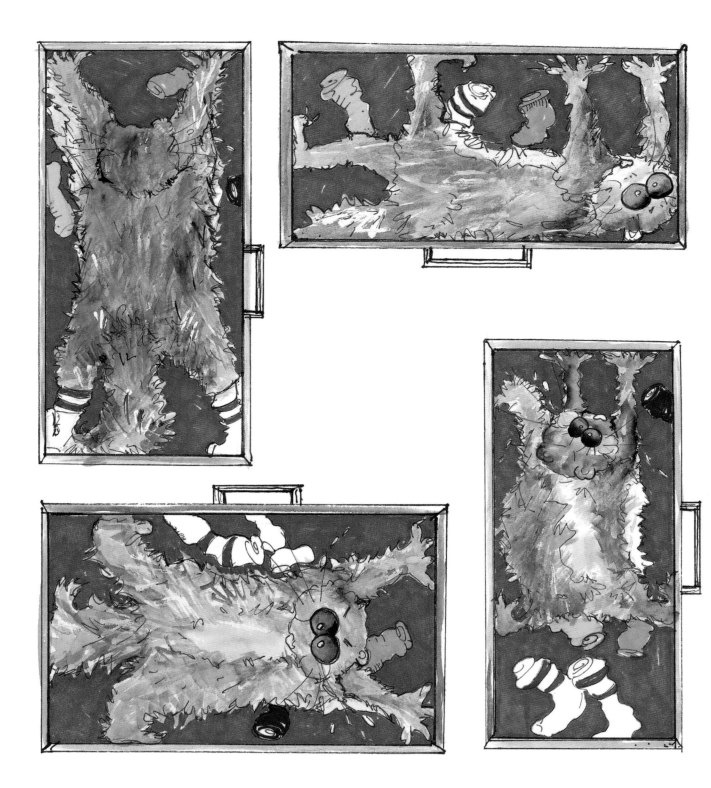

"Pushing here, pushing there,
In the corners and everywhere,
With my body, I nudge and nudge
But this drawer will not budge!"

"Don't worry, Al, don't be blue.
I am coming to rescue you.

"I'll push and push on the door.
Then I'll help you open that drawer.

"Oh my dear, the door is locked.
Oh no, Al, my way is blocked!"

"Come, Kitty, come. Socks to put away.
Come, Kitty, come. No time to play.

"Now be good. No more jumping.
You must be careful; it's me you're bumping!"

"Naughty Kitty! Look at what you've done!
Getting knocked down isn't much fun!

"Now the socks are on the floor,
When they should be in the drawer!"

"That drawer is open! I can't believe my eyes.
From my sock drawer has sprung a surprise!

"How did it get there? Where will it go?
Besides, what is it? I really do not know."

"Sal, I'm trapped . . . trapped I am!
Help, Sal, help! I need to scram.

"Kitty has me cornered. I'm his prey!
Sal, please come and save the day!"

"Sal, leap down from that windowsill.
Kitty's coming closer, even closer still.

"Sal, do you hear my frightened tune?
Hurry now, and do something soon."

Maddie yells, "Kitty, you must stay back!
Our little visitor is scared of your attacks.

"How he got here, I must wonder.
Poor thing, shaking like there's thunder.

"Kitty, stop hissing. Go, Kitty! Shooooo!
Frightened furry friend, what are you?"

"Stay back Kitty, you must behave.
Our little visitor is trying to be brave.

"Don't worry, little one, don't you fret.
You'll soon be free of this Kitty's threat.

"Now run tiny friend, out the open door.
Return to the woods, to play and explore."

"Back with your friend, now you're alright.
So sorry Kitty gave you such a fright.

"But *who* are you and *what* are you?
Can't you give me one small clue?

"You look like a squirrel but you have little flaps.
Are you a bat or a rodent perhaps?"

"Thank you, thank you, for setting me free!
Now I can return home happily.

"'*Who* are we and *what* are we,' asks our lady pal.
I am Al and this is Sal.

"With our wide flaps and eyes like black pearls,
We are special . . . we're flying squirrels!"

Maddie's amazement she could not disguise.
These little creatures were such a surprise.

She looks and wonders about her furry guests.
"What are flying squirrels?" Once more she requests.

"You're ready to leave, ready to roam.
Ready to return to your forest home."

"But what makes you special? That was my request.
Without this answer, I shall not rest!"

"Listen closely and we'll answer your plea.
We'll share our story quite gladly.
Flying squirrels are very special creatures
With lots of important physical features.

"We have special eyes.
No, they're not a disguise.
We're nocturnal, you see,
We eat and play at night, very happily.

"We have a home high in the trees.
Eating seeds and berries in the breeze!
Fruits and eggs are hard to beat.
And insects make a yummy treat."

"Our special tail is flat and wide.
Helps us steer, helps us glide.
Moves us up, moves us down.
Side-to-side and all around.

"We have flaps; they're folds of skin
That help us soar and make us grin.
From branch to branch, and here and there.
We parachute gracefully through the air."

"It is nice to meet you, my special friends.
But tonight, our adventure must come to an end."

"When Kitty and I look out the door,
We will always remember the secret drawer!"

Author's Note

The inspiration for this book came from my cat, Odis, who sat for two long days in front of my sock drawer. Although my husband and I had no idea why, Odis just watched and waited for the secret inside to be revealed. On the second day, we opened the drawer, and this story unfolded before our eyes.

Out came this flying animal. We wondered, "How did this strange animal get into the house? How did it get into my sock drawer? What exactly was it?" We learned that it is a remarkable flying squirrel and figured out that it must have gotten in through the door left open by the painter, just like in the story.

As the years passed, our flying squirrel and his mate returned to the woods near our creek again and again, year after year. One year our unusual guests nestled in a basket on our porch and in that basket a litter of baby flying squirrels was born! To this day, we watch and wait for our flying squirrel friends to return each year.

N.G.
Orland Park, IL
2014

NANCY GEE, Author, expresses her love of nature while stirring the imaginations and hearts of children of all ages. This is her first picture book and she looks forward to continuing with her writing. Nancy lives in Orland Park, Illinois with her husband. She is Owner and President of Maywood Industries, Inc., a company that manufactures specialty crating and sells building materials throughout the Chicagoland area. Nancy is a graduate of Drake University.

RAYE ANN SAUNORIS, Illustrator, is a professional artist, muralist and designer. She is the founder and owner of "A Raye of Color." Raye Ann's work embraces everyone through various art forms. She resides in the southwest suburbs of Chicago with her husband and two children. She has been a preschool teacher at the Farm and Nature Pre-school in Palos Park, Illinois.